T0062995

Myths and Archetypes in
Garo (A·chik) Folk Narratives

Myths and Archetypes in Garo (A·chik) Folk Narratives

LUCY R. MARAK

PARTRIDGE
A Penguin Random House Company

To order additional copies of this book, contact
Partridge India
000 800 10062 62
orders.india@partridgepublishing.com

www.partridgepublishing.com/india

This work is dedicated…

To my
beloved father, the Late Mr. Francis Cheran
who valued art and education and
inculcated the same in me!

Foreword

This work is revised version of the Thesis submitted by the author to the North Eastern Hill University, for which, she was awarded the degree of the Doctor of Philosophy in the department of English.

Ever since the first contact of the Europeans with the Garos in the second half of the 18th century, there had been spurt of interests among the European and later Indian Administrators and Scholars in studying and doing researches on various aspects of Garo life and culture. Out of the multitude of the publications, mention can be made of John Eliot's "Observations on the inhabitations of Garrow Hills made during a public deputation in the years 1788-89"; Hamilton's "An account of Assam, 1808-09"; A. White's "A Memoir of Late David Scot," 1832; A. Playfair's "The Garos", 1909; Robbins Burling's "Rengsanggre"; 1963, Chie Nakane's "Garo and Khasi", 1961; Erik de Maaker's "Negotiating Life", etc.

Mr. Dewansing Rongmithu's Monumental works like: "The Folktales of the Garos", 1960 and "Epic Lore of the Garos", 1967 and "Apasong Agana", 1970 evoked further interests among the scholars.

The establishment of North-Eastern Hill University Campus at Tura opened up wider avenues for more in-depth studies and researches on the life, customs and cultures of the Garos. The University campus being located in Tura, the whole Garo Hills were wide open for their field works. With such facilities wide open before them, the students took the advantage in going all out for unearthing the past. As a result, hectic researches have been going on in the NEHU Campus, Tura. Some of these research works have been published, mention of which can be made of Dr. (Ms) Semeri Alva B. Sangma's "Rites of Passage in Garo Oral Literature", 2012 and "Dakokni Sul", 2013 edited by Prof. Caroline R. Marak - a contributor of articles in different journals and magazine.

Dr. (Sister) Lucy R. Marak's work is also one of such products. Being a Sister of the Roman Catholic Religious order, she had multiple charitable works, besides her teaching assignment in the Tura Don Bosco College. Yet whatever time was available to her, she grabbed the opportunity to do research on the topic, "Myths and Archetypes in Garo Folk Narratives", for which she obtained her Ph. D. Degree. Being born and brought up within the Garo cultural milieu, she had the advantage in understanding the myths and archetypes narrated to her orally by the most knowledgeable old people of different villages in the far-flung areas of Garo Hills. Therefore, this work is the product of the studies of all the earlier publications and the field works. She has collected the myths, charms and chants and all other information from the mouth of the narrators and as such, it is authentic and authoritative.

It is from this point of view that I commend this book to both the scholars and the general readers.

Dated: Tura
The 15th January, 2014

Dr. Milton S. Sangma

Former Pro-Vice Chancellor,
NEHU, Tura-Campus
Present Pro-Vice Chancellor,
ICFAI University, Meghalaya

Preface

*T*he whole process of completing this thesis has been enlightening and an enriching one. I turn to God Almighty in humble obeisance for the numerous graces and blessings I received during the course of this work. The writing of this thesis has helped me to deepen my understanding of myths and archetypes in Garo (A·chik) Folk Narratives and it has inculcated in me love and appreciation for my own culture. It has enabled me to discover the rich cultural heritage and traditions. This study has convinced me of the fact that our forefathers were god fearing people.

The present book is a revised version of the doctoral thesis I submitted to the North Eastern Hill University (NEHU), Tura Campus, Tura, Meghalaya in August 2012. The original dissertation was entitled: "Myths and archetypes in Garo (A·chik) Folk Narratives: A Select Study." It is revised for publication sake only.

Many people have contributed generously towards the writing of this book. Prof. Jyotirmoy Prodhani has played a vital role in making this work see the light of day. He graciously accepted to supervise my research, and made necessary suggestions and corrections during the course of the research and above all for his keen interest in the topic. I appreciate the interest and cooperation of his family members as well. I cannot but say a sincere thanks to Prof. Caroline R. Marak, the Joint Supervisor, for her valuable suggestions and for taking pains to go through my work. My sincere gratitude to Prof. Sujata Gurudev, Head, Department of English, NEHU, Tura Campus, Mr R. S. Thakur for his timely advice and suggestions, Dr. Angela Ingty and Dr. Fameline K. Marak, who, inspite of their tremendous work load spared their valuable time to go through my work, and for making the necessary corrections. My sincere gratitude goes also to the Teaching and Non-teaching staff of the Departments of English and Garo of NEHU, Tura Campus.

My sincere and heartfelt thanks to Dr. Milton S Sangma, former Vice-Chancellor, NEHU, Tura Campus, Present Pro-Vice Chancellor ICFAI University, Meghalaya for the valuable suggestions he offered me when I began the studies and now for writing the Foreward for the book.

I owe a debt of gratitude to Dr. (Fr) Joy Kachappilly SDB for patiently and minutely going through the entire thesis, making necessary corrections and for suggesting improvements. I also thank the former Principals of Don Bosco College Rev. Fr. V. A. Cyriac SDB, for allowing me to pursue the research and Rev. Fr. Alex Mathew SDB, for his encouragement and for granting me leave from College, whenever it was required.

I would like to place on record my heartfelt thanks to Rev. Sr. Pyngrope Rosa, my Provincial Superior, FMA Province of Shillong for granting me the necessary permission to undertake this study and for her continued encouragement and support. I feel it my grave and bounded duty to express my sincere word of gratitude to Rev. Sr. Phyllis Bamon, the sisters and the inmates of Auxilium Tura and Margaret Bosco Girls' Hostel, for releasing me from my duty thus enabling me to complete my research.

To all my friends who have been a source of inspiration, and pillar of support in the course of my study, I say thanks. The numerous silent services rendered to me by them cannot go unacknowledged, therefore, my special thanks to all of them for standing by me at all times and for their ever willingness to help me in this endeavour of mine especially Dr. L. K. Gracy and Rev. Fr. Albert T. Sangma SDB who willingly and generously helped out in getting ready the text, to my colleagues at Don Bosco College, especially of the Department of English, for their support, encouragement, and love which kept me going.

Special thanks to the Library Staff, NEHU, Tura Campus, and of NEHU, Shillong, for their availability and generous service to procure the needed books and materials. I cannot forget the Teaching, Non-Teaching and the Library Staff of Don Bosco College.

My special thanks to my sister Dr. (Mrs) Anju R. Marak and Dr. D K. Brahma MD, who have been meeting the expenses of this publication. Finally the manager and the staff of Patridge Publishers deserve my gratitude for printing this book. May God bless everyone.

Last but not the least, I am really indebted and wish to express my special thanks to my family members – my late father, my mother, brothers and sisters and their family members, nieces and nephews, relatives and well wishers for being supportive to my undertakings.

Lucy R. Marak

Contents

Chapter IV

Chapter I

Introduction

The Garo (*A·chik*) folk narratives have a rich legacy. There are so many elements and patterns which form the narrative of the folk literature of the Garos[1]. Most of these narratives are in oral form and they continue to survive down the generations being alive only through oral renditions and community memories. Interestingly, these narratives have significantly shaped and governed the cultural consciousness of the *A·chiks*. The *A·chiks*, being a community with intimate proximity to nature and its mystical manifestations, invented a rich heritage of folklore and narratives by aligning the mystical as well as the innocent with the experiential comprehension of their

---

[1] The origin of the name Garo is a conjecture. Different views are expressed on the meaning of the word, 'Garo'. The tribe itself is known to outsiders as 'Garo' but the Garos call themselves, *'A·chik mande'* or 'hill men'. There are two theories on this point. The first suggests the word to be corrupted from 'Gara' to 'Garo'. It could also be a corrupt form of one of the sub-tribes of the Garos, 'Gara-Ganching'. Another theory is that 'Garo' is either a development of 'Dura' or a corruption of it. The educated Garos of today like to call themselves only as *A·chik* rather than by their divisional names (Playfair, 1998, 7-8).

immediate reality into the folk narratives that matured with time into abiding community beliefs.

The term 'Folklore' was first suggested by a British antiquarian, William Thoms, in 1846. He realized that scholarly work on materials of folklore was being carried on under various names such as 'Popular Antiquities' or 'Popular Literature' and therefore needed to be categorized with single label to designate this important area of enquiry. He, therefore, suggested "a good Saxon Compound Folk – Lore – *the lore of the people*" to replace all other somewhat cumbersome terms, in a letter to the *Athenaeum* (see Jawaharlal Handoo, 2000, 1).

Handoo, however, observes that folklore had been studied with scholarly interest long before Thoms coined the term. Though Thoms coined this term, he did not give a definition of folklore. But he certainly had some kind of specific view of folklore in mind. His words and phrases such as 'manners', 'customs', 'neglected customs', 'fading legends', 'fragmentary ballads', etc., do present a clear picture of his increasing awareness of folklore which was "closely associated with nineteenth century intellectual currents of romanticism and nationalism" (Dundes, 1965, p.v).

While defining folklore, Handoo observes that there is no common framework to categorize folklore of various cultures. This has been the guiding principle for collection, classification, indexing, archiving and, above all, interpretations and analyses of folklore data all over the world. Some cultures may be rich in terms of some genre as the *marchen* (folktale) is a strong genre of Indo-European cultures owing to various geo-cultural factors. Handoo mentions how various types of changed or transformed *marchen* can be found among the American Indians, South and Central African cultures and in Asia (see Handoo, 2000, 10).

However, despite these characteristics of genres and the analytical categories, folklore has been defined differently by different scholars. These definitions not only try to define the folkloric phenomenon, but also try to list the genres of which this phenomenon is made of. Naturally, the weaknesses inherent in these definitions gave rise to controversies, and these, as expected, centred on the same old problem, that is, the problem of trying to draw line between cultural anthropology and folklore studies. Within these definitions, and outside them in the wider academic circles – both of anthropology and of folklore there was at least one thing on which, by and large, all seemed to agree, and that is folk literature or to use William R. Bascom's term 'verbal art' (1955,245-52). Scholars generally seem to be in agreement that verbal art or folk literature is folklore and is a separate area of inquiry, different from cultural anthropology.

Abrams in his *A Glossary of Literary Terms* writes that folklore has been the collective name applied to 'sayings, verbal compositions, and social rituals' which are handed down mostly orally and not necessarily in written form. According to him folklore includes legends, superstitions, songs, tales, proverbs, riddles, spells, and nursery rhymes; pseudoscientific lore about the weather, plants, and animals; customary activities at births, marriages, and deaths; and traditional dances and forms of drama performed on holidays or at communal gatherings (Abrams, 2008, 104-105).

Bess Lomax Hawes says:

> Folklore is an unfinished profession, a profession within which there are still many areas of argument and conflict, a profession within which individuals

> still have serious choices to make. And just as the individual folklorist is required by virtue to his membership within the profession – to balance out the conflicting essentials of his work, so too is the discipline of folklore itself (qtd. in Handoo, *et al*, 1999, 1).

Handoo in his *Theoretical Essays in Indian Foklore* elaborates the theory and practice of folklore. He opines that Grimms of Germany, known as the founding fathers of folklore studies, had interests both in folklore and languages. Their interest in folklore remained, for some time, subordinate to their linguistic (philological) investigations, which, strictly speaking, has not concerned itself with the problems of meaning. In fact, the paradigm of philology is essentially a paradigm of reconstruction, and has remained heavily loaded with European ethnocentrism. Even after the release from this subordination, the main concern of Grimms' (particularly by Jacob's) effort was to collect parallels and try to reconstruct the original forms of folklore items. This demanded a reasonable collection of data and particularly rich and fascinating fairy tales. Thus Grimms finally ended up as the greatest collector of folktales. Grimms' efforts laid the foundation of a new discipline and certainly a theoretical framework which eventually was picked up by Max Muller and European contemporaries. Though Max Muller did not deviate that Grimm's methodology yet he added folkloristic dimensions to the philological model and took as Handoo put it, "beyond the objective of reconstruction into the realm of meaning" (see Handoo, 2000, 45).

Handoo also mentions how Theoder Benfey, an Indologist like Max Muller, centred his attention on the problems of diffusion and migration of folklore. He gradually enfolded the field of theory and methodology of folklore scholarship. Benfey added one more historically important dimension to the folklore theories of the nineteenth century: those similarities of folklore items across the continents and unrelated cultures could now be explained with the help of historical factors such as migration and the resultant borrowing. Benfey's theoretical contribution was a natural by-product of a larger theoretical bias: that the source of all folktales of the world was India, which, however was never proved. His theory of borrowing might have indirectly contributed to the fresh thinking on atomistic bias in folklore theory (Handoo, ibid, 47).

The Finnish or historic-geographic method placed much emphasis on form which was considered as the sole criterion for achieving the objective of tracing the original form and travel routes of a tale or any other item of folklore. It certainly emphasized mathematical accuracy in analytical procedures thus minimizing the chances of imaginative speculation which was being applied in an unrestrained manner in folklore scholarship. This method also inspired the creation of valuable folk narrative lexicons such as the *Type Index* and the *Motif Index*, and also opened up the possibilities of the use of computers in folklore studies (Thompson, 1955-58, vol. 6). Modern structuralists seem to have borrowed at least the language of analysis from the *Finnish* method despite the strange irony that structuralism in folklore studies was born as a reaction to *Finnish* methodology and diachronic studies (Propp, 1928, 15).

Structuralism in folklore was born out of Russian Formalist thought and as a reaction to *Finnish* methodology and diachronic studies. Vladimir Propp was one of the major proponents of *Russian Formalism* that had short period of development. Through the publication of *Morphology of the Folktale* (1968) he became the first structural folklorist.

The original Russian version of Propp's work was published in 1928, but it remained unknown to the English speaking world for almost thirty years. The Formalist School was officially condemned from within and with no communication with the outside world. Threatened by these crises, Propp himself had to abandon Formalism and morphological analysis in order to devote himself to historical and comparative research on the relationship between oral literature and myth, rites and institutions.

Propp's method of measuring the morphological elements of fairy tales and ignoring the content and context can be compared with that brand of linguistic structuralism which paid attention exclusively to the rules which governed the construction of statements, and in the process Formalism lost sight of the fact that 'no language exists in which vocabulary can be deduced from the syntax.' The study of any linguistic system requires the combined effort of a grammarian and the philologist. "Thus for oral tradition" writes Levi-Strauss, "morphology is sterile unless ethnographic observation, direct or indirect, comes to fertilize it" (qtd. in Handoo, 2000, 50).

Scholars of structural analysis, drawing inspiration from the French anthropological school and nourished by the experiments of Levi-Strauss with American Indian mythology, separated itself completely from Formalism. They claim to have made the discovery of the mythological truth in the unity of concrete and the abstract. Form is defined in contrast to content; however, they also claimed that structure had no content. According to Strauss, "it is the content comprehended in a logical organization which is conceived of as a property of reality." These scholars therefore believe that the Proppian analysis deals with form alone whereas Levi-Straussian structuralism takes care of both form and content. Besides, Propp's morphological analysis is based on Russian fairy tales (*marchen*) alone while Strauss is trying to uncover the realm of the myths. Propp does not alter the 'syntax' of the tale; in other words, he attempts to decipher its morphology (functions of the characters) and the combinations as it is 'given' by the informant. Levi Strauss on the other hand, believes that the content of a myth narrative comprehended in a logical organization cannot and should not lie on the given structure and therefore needs 're-arrangement' by reducing the structural components to meaningful paradigms.

Levi-Strauss draws heavily upon the linguistic theory of Ferdinand de Saussare, Trobetskoy and Roman Jakobson. His firm belief in Freudian concepts that 'genuine meaning lies behind the apparent one,' that 'no meaning has to be accepted at its face value,' that the 'true meaning... is not that of which men are aware,' and that 'conscious data are always erroneous or illusory,' clearly shows that he looks at 'conscious meaning' something outside the scope of his structural analysis (Fenichel, 1945, 4). The structural analysis of Levi-Strauss tells, how myths are created at the unconscious level, but it does not tell us why they survive, and are remembered and believed by human societies irrespective of the changes that have occurred to mankind. It would seem that his structural analysis is more concerned about the uniform biological functioning of the human mind rather than the logical working of the human societies. His formulations have certainly added a new dimension to folkloristic research, that is, it has enhanced the depths of 'savage mind' (Levi-Strauss, 1962, 10).

The psychoanalytical school was influenced by the extraordinary writings of Sigmund Freud, the father of psychoanalysis. Their explorations were mainly based on dreams and their dreamers. With the help of the dream, psychologists always attempt translating the dreams from the unconscious fantasy to a conscious meaningful symbolic phenomenon. A dream is largely an abstract experience of an individual. The myth on the other hand, is invariably shared by collective psyche of the ethnic group, sometimes by all the members of a culture or even a nation (Handoo, 2000, 54). The problem of genre and the generic qualities and the relationship between the genres have been completely ignored by the folklorists who follow psychoanalytic method.

1.2. Folklore and Oral History

James Morrison once famously said, "All societies have a history and all history begins as oral" (Morrison, 1998). It offers a challenge to the accepted myths of history. With complete reliance on the written document, the paradigm of history becomes inevitably a prisoner of the idiosyncratic written testimony that has been created to survive. But spoken word would be evanescent, it is fluid, dynamic, like a river in which thoughts and experiences are presented as a spontaneous process connected by grammatical structures (Handoo et al, 1999, 4). In contrast, the written word is static; it fixes thoughts and experiences as products. The distance in dialogical process has enough possibilities for false presentations and distortions. One must also keep in mind that the paradigms of written history and written literature have coexisted. It is not surprising to see the aspects of written history influencing many other important aspects (art, architecture, dress, cuisine, etc) of a culture by virtue of the hegemony of the writing system.

One must also remember that writing is not merely a tool, a medium through which we manifest our thoughts. It is a practice that alters human consciousness. It is a different way of perceiving the world and conducting the affairs of the world.

Historians claim that history is an ongoing dialogue between the present and the past to understand the future. When the past is presented falsely, it automatically influences the present and plans equally a false future. The historians, who are guided by the concept of chronology, must be aware of the sequence of cause and effect otherwise, the historical analysis is faulty.

The historical documentation of the kings, palaces and their life styles has been, it would seem, the ultimate goal of history writing in India and elsewhere but when extending to the tribal situations, the documented referent is missing, as tribal people have no written texts, no written history and no palaces.

A folk epic, strictly speaking, is not history, but its underlying metaphor. If interpreted accurately and trusted, it can tell us about the real history of an ethnic group, a speech community or even a region. Other genres of folklore which scholars discard as 'false' or 'exaggerated' can be useful in tracing the history of the tribe. The tribal people did not develop the kind of social structure, caste system and its hierarchies, or the feudalism we generally notice among the non-tribal population of India. So the ethnographic facts should be measured by tribal standards which certainly are oral and free from constraints and the hegemony of written metaphors.

1.3. Four Sectors of Folklore and Folk Life Studies

M. Dorson in his book, *Folklore and Folk life: An Introduction* (1972) has outlined four broad sectors of folklore and folk life studies. These are:

a) Oral literature
b) Material culture
c) Social folk custom, and
d) Performing folk arts

1.3.1. Oral Literature

Folk narratives include many other categories of oral lore. Oral literatures, called verbal art of expressive literature, are "spoken, sung, and voiced forms of traditional utterances" (Dorson, 1972, 2). Oral narrative has its own manifold distinctions like myth, fairy tale or *marchen*, romantic tale or novella, religious tale, folktale, legend, animal tale, anecdote, joke, numskull tale etc.

A major subdivision of folk narrative is oral poetry or folk poetry. This too has its own family of related forms. For example, Handoo says that folk epics, ballads, folksongs, lullabies, work songs and songs associated with ritual and rites (Samskaras), such as birth, marriage and death are commonly found in almost all parts of India.

Proverbs and riddles are also important parts of oral literature and they are highly structured set forms of oral literary forms. Unlike prose narrative forms and oral poetry, proverbs and riddles do not show much multiple existences. Proverbs and proverbial expressions have formed an inseparable part of the written literatures throughout the world; riddles have stayed in the folk life and functions as important devices of imparting knowledge about cultural semantics, folk logic and the culturally ethical behaviour the younger members of societies are to follow.

Folk Speech, as Dorson observes, "Embraces the local and regional turns of phrase that deviate from the standard language" (qtd. in Handoo, 2000, 14), which is usually taught in schools in an informal manner. One of the main characteristics of folk speech is that it is more restricted to oral circulation. He further observes that these words or expressions may be taboo words or expressions. They may be a kind of passive vocabulary. Moreover, these characteristics of folk speech are not only limited to vocabulary but they exist at the level of grammar, idiom and phonetics as well. For example, slang in this respect is folk speech. Besides these major forms of oral literatures, there are other minor forms which also fall under the above sector. These are chants, prayers, laments, cries and even hollers.

1.3.2. Material Culture

In contrast to verbal art or oral folklore, physical folklore generally is called material culture. According to Dorson:

> Material culture responds to techniques, skills, recipes and formulas transmitted across the generations and subject to the same forces of conservative tradition and individual variation as verbal art (qtd. in Handoo, 2000, 14).

This aspect of folklore and folk life is visible rather than aural. Material culture is concerned with the issues like how tradition-oriented societies construct their homes following the traditional norms of folk housing, how people make their clothes, prepare their food, farm and fish, process the earth's bounty, fashion their tools and implements and design their furniture and utensil, etc.

One of the most interesting and fascinating aspects of material culture of India is its arts and crafts. These arts have followed a definite continuity in the history of folk arts of this country. Yet these art forms have not received the attention they deserve and are still in a state of utter neglect. Many of our prestigious old museums and archives do not have a corner for these traditional art forms. It is only recently that some attention has been given to preserve these forms of art. Folk arts and crafts, as is well known, are objects of material culture that simultaneously give pleasure and serve some political, social and economic end.

According to Glassie:

> If a pleasure-giving function predominates it is called craft ... the interior of a house is designed primarily to be used and its function may be classed primarily as economic; its exterior is designed primarily to be seen, and its function may be classed as primarily as aesthetic (Glassie, 1972, 153-280).

1.3.3. Social Folk Customs

Another important area of folklore and folk life studies, very close to material culture, is the field of social customs. It emphasizes more on group interaction and individual skills and performances as secondary. Investigations in this area are more centred on the family and community observances of the people living in the villages, tribal belts and even the industrial areas of Indian cities. Of particular importance are the rites of passage connected with birth, initiation, marriage, death and similar rites. Oral literature is constituted by the songs, tales and the aspects associated with the rites and the social folk customs by studying the social custom and ritualistic observances.

Similarly, Handoo observes that the ritual and custom associated with the festivals, such as *Holi*, *Dipavali* in northern and central India, *Durga Puja* in the east and south, *Gauri-Ganapati* in the west coast, *Pongal* and *Onam* in deep South and hundreds of similar festivals also form an important segment of Social Folk Customs. These festivals, just like the folk rites, may have literary as well as ritualistic aspect. Most of these festivals in our country seem to be embedded with agricultural activity and, therefore, follow a calendrical cycle. There are thousands of little customs and ritualistic practices being observed by Indian village folks for the sake of rains, agricultural prosperity and for warding off natural calamities such as floods, famines, etc.

The religious aspect of social folk customs in India is multidimensional and highly complex. The processes of intense acculturation and the survival of indigenous cultural traits can be seen in the *Bhutta* and *Teyyam* worship in the south-west coastal India. Many tribal groups do not maintain close contacts with the firmly established mainstream religious practices but the maintenance of indigenous modes of worship have been preserved carefully. Similar indigenous traits are also prevalent in the worship of *Bathou* by the Bodos, *Mastan*, *Joka* and other deities by the Koch Rajbongsis.

1.3.4. Performing Folk Arts

According to Handoo, the fourth and the last sector of folklore and folk life studies may be designated as the Performing Folk Arts. This sector primarily concerns traditional music, dance and drama. According to this school, all items of folklore, when delivered are performed. However, performance here in its traditional sense strictly means the conscious presentation of these arts – dance, drama, folk music, etc., by individuals or groups who carry these art forms from one generation to another.

One of the most important areas of this sector is the traditional music, which is passed on from one person to another and is performed from memory rather than through written or printed musical score. Folk dance, folk drama, dance-drama, oral poetry, ritual and prayers always carry some element of music in them.

The traditional musical instruments are also of equal importance. Musical instruments are embedded with respective musical form. A particular kind of folk music is at times identified by its instrument. The area of Indian folk dances is very vast. Most of the time folk music and folk dances go together and share many important characteristics. Folk drama is another important field in the performing folk arts sector. Drama of any sort calls for the play world by the players generally through the use of masks, costumes, and a special area for playing. The traditions of Indian folk drama are very ancient and rooted in Indian religion and ritual. Most of the forms of Indian folk drama are associated with ritual and festival and have close affinity with music and dance.

Many fascinating forms of Indian music and dance are, however, linked with what now being labeled as dance-drama and recognized as such as a kind of a new genre on the assumption that it contains the elements of both the dance and the drama. The elements of dance and music are inseparable part of Indian folk drama.

1.4. Narrative

A narrative or story is a construct created in a suitable format (written, spoken, poetry, prose, images, song, theatre or dance) that describes a sequence of fictional or non-fictional events. Shlomith Rimmon-Kenan defines *narrative fiction* as 'the narration of a succession of fictional events'. Many today take 'narrative' to mean 'a mode of knowledge' or a 'cognitive scheme' by which we perceive and interpret the world. Such a view does not necessarily stem from narratology. It can be seen as rooted in the etymology of 'narrative', originating in the Sanskrit *gna* and coming into English via the Latin *gnarus*, indicating the "signifiers associated with the passing on of knowledge by one who knows" (Rimmon-Kenan, 2006, 14).

The term 'narrative' suggests the existence of competing 'truths', each carrying persuasion for the group upholding it. Moreover, as Kenan points out, it implies that each version is not a neutral account of events, but an attempt to naturalize an ideological stance (ibid, 2006, 12).

Kenan points out those narrative versions are not ideologically neutral; however they attempt to neutralize it. The term 'narrative' was used to designate at least two different concepts: what the Russian Formalists called *fabula*, that is, the abstracted events in the order of their presumed 'occurrence', and what they called *sjuzet*, that is, the organization of these events in the text. In the sense of *fabula*, narrative is medium-independent, though narratologists disagree on whether it should be seen as raw material for textual elaboration or as a construct, abstracted from the text. Be it as it may, 'narrative' in this sense was 'always already' open to shaping in different media. As early as 1966, Barthes said in his *Introduction to the Structural Analysis of Narrative*:

> Narrative is first and foremost a prodigious variety of genres, themselves distributed among different substances – as though any material were fit to receive man's stories. Able to be carried by articulated language, spoken or written, fixed or moving images, gestures, and the ordered mixture of all these substances; narrative is present in myth, legend, fable, tale, novella, epic, history, tragedy, drama, comedy, mime, painting […]stained glass windows, cinema, comics, news items, conversation (Engl. transl. 1977, 79).

Roland Barthes, one of the most significant narrative theorists, broadens the realm of narrative theory by employing the methods of structural linguists. He places narratives at the level of discourse arguing that "narrative is present in every age, in every place, in every society; it begins with the very history of mankind and there nowhere is nor have been a people without narrative. All classes, all human groups, have their narratives" (1977, 79).

Whereas 'narrative' as *fabula* is medium-independent and hence amenable to shaping in different media, 'narrative' as *sjuzet* was originally conceived as language-bound and therefore found its way into other disciplines concerned with verbal articulation. However, narrative as *sjuzet* was originally understood as artistic composition. However, in other disciplines it is seen as a 'composition' or 'organization' without the qualifier 'artistic'. Thus, Hayden

White distinguishes between annals, chronicles, and narrative history as manifestations of degrees of narrative organization. The organizing features, he enumerates, being 'a central subject', 'well marked beginning, middle, and end', 'peripeteia', an 'identifiable narrative voice', 'coherence', 'closure', and 'the impulse to moralize reality' (1981). People are fascinated with narratives, because in them "reality wears the mask of a meaning, the completeness and fullness of which we can only imagine, but never experience" (White, 1981, 20). Coherence also plays a central role in Peter Brooks' description of the psychoanalyst's reshaping of the fragmentary stories presented by analysand: "First of all, the psychoanalyst is ever concerned with the stories told by his patients, who are patients precisely because of the weakness of the narrative discourses that they present: the incoherence, inconsistency, and lack of explanatory force in the way they tell their lives" (Peter Brooks, 1994, 47). And again, this time explicitly in terms of *fabula* and *sjuzet*, in his discussion of *Law's Stories*: "The courtroom lawyer's task would seem to be to take an often fragmentary and confusing *fabula* and turn it into a seamless, convincing *sjuzet*" (Rimmon-Kenan, 2006, 14).

There have also been attempts to define *narrative* in terms of a *communicative* framework. The term *narration* has also been defined in terms of *communication*. In the *communicative* framework, a narrative is viewed in terms of a *transaction* which has an *addresser*, *addressee* and a *message* (Rimmon-Kenan, 2009, 2).

In the spirit of Genette's distinction between 'histoire', 'recit' and 'narration' (1972, 71-6), Rimmon-Kenan labels these aspects as 'story', 'text' and 'narration' respectively. 'Story' designates the narrated events, abstracted from their disposition in the text and reconstructed in their chronological order together with the participants in these events. Whereas 'story' is a succession of events, 'text' is a spoken or written discourse which undertakes their telling. The act or process of production is the third aspect – 'narration'. Narration can be considered as both real and fictional. Within the text, communication involves a fictional narrator transmitting a narrative to a fictional narratee. It is only through the text that he or she acquires knowledge of the story and of the narration (Rimmon-Kenan 2009, 3-4).

Tzvetan Todorov (1969) coined the term 'narratology' for the structuralist analysis of any given narrative into its constituent parts to determine their function(s) and relationships. For these purposes, the story is what is narrated usually with chronological order of themes, motives and plot lines, or what is sometimes called 'natural chronology'. The minute there is more than one character, events may become simultaneous and the story is often multilinear rather than unilinear.[2]

The main types of discrepancy between story-order and text-order called '*anachronies*' (Genette, 1972, 265) which are traditionally known as 'flashback' or 'retrospection' on the one hand and 'foreshadowing' or 'anticipation' on the other. Genette also uses the term '*analepsis*' and '*prolepsis*'. An *analepsis* is a narration of a story-event at a point in the text after later events have been told, a *prolepsis* is a narration

---

[2]   Strict linear chronology, then, is neither natural nor an actual characteristic of most stories. It is a conventional 'norm' which has become as widespread as to replace the actual mutlilinear temporarily of the story and acquire a pseudo-natural status. Causality can either be implied by chronology or gain an explicit status in its own right (Rimmon-Kenan, 2009, 17).

of a story-event at a point before earlier events have been mentioned (Genette, 1972, 90).

According to Genette (1972), *Analepsis* provide past information either about the character, event or story-line mentioned at that point in the text (homodiegetic analepsis) or about another character, event, or story-line (heterodiegetic analepsis). *Prolepses* are much less frequent than *analepses*[3]; they can refer either to the same character, event, or story-line figuring at that point in the text (homodiegetic) or to another character, event, or story-line (heterodiegetic). They can like *analepses*, cover either a period beyond the end of the first narrative (external), or a period anterior to it but posterior to the point at which it is narrated (internal), or combine both (mixed) (Rimmon-Kenan, 2009, 49).

A narrative can be *sociologically* defined. However, the features or factors must be of sociological consequence, reflect social patterns, or are activated by social factors.

Aside from the sociological definition, narrative has also been *cognitively* defined, but the factors are looked at from a psychological perspective. In a sense, every aspect of narrative, and narrative as a whole, cannot be understood or even sensed unless they have been cognitively processed. So the cognitive approach is implicit in narrative studies,

---

[3] Both these *analepsis*, though one is *homodiegetic* and one *heterodiegetic*, evoke past which precedes the starting point of the first narrative and hence they are 'external analepses'. Other *analepses* may conjure up a past which 'occurred' after the starting point of the first narrative but is either repeated analeptically or narrated for the first time at a point in the text later than the place where it is 'due' is known as 'internal analepses'.

even if it is not always systematically brought to the surface in the analysis of narrative.

Much valuable research on narrative has been done by literary scholars. However, there is no such a thing as a *literary* definition of narrative. It does seem to be the case that definitions of narrative in literature could easily be applied to spheres outside literature. Thus, an absolute distinction between literature and other spheres of human activity, even if one concentrates on what appears to be a specifically 'literary' concept such as *narrative*, cannot be made.

The *human* element in narrative is important. We can say here that narrative must have a *human* (or *human like*) agent who must do something or something must be done to him or her. Even stories involving animals or inanimate objects have *characters* which act like, or have features of human beings. The *human* factor can be regarded as a *paradigmatic core feature* of narrative.

Movement is also essential to narrative. A static description cannot be a narrative. Thus *verbs of movement* are more essential to narrative than verbs which describe states. At a more informal level, we can view what are sometimes called *dynamic verbs* (i.e. verbs which describe physical activity) as being essential to narrative.

There are some scholars who claim that the *storyteller* is necessary for a narrative. But the *storyteller* and its importance need further specification, as there are some stories which do not have a well-defined *storyteller*, and there may be several *storytellers* in a narrative.

Ross Murfin and Supiya M. Roy say that a narrative may be a story or telling of a story, or an account of a situation or event. The narratives may be fictional or true; they may be written in either prose or verse (2003, 287).

Livia Polanyi the author of the book *Telling the American Story* (1991) defines narrative as:

> Stories and past time reports are specific, affirmative, past time narratives which tell about a series of events which took place at specific unique moments in a unique past time world.

Anna – Leena Siikala, a folklorist and an anthropologist of religion, defines narrative in the following manner:

> A narrative is embarked on either in reply to some external stimulus, such as request from the audience, or so that the narrator may express something he considers important, amusing or otherwise worth telling. The performance of a narrative is a logical, goal-oriented act carried out in a state of interaction. The narrator may aim to entertain, to teach, to warn or to criticize his listener. He may also tell his story as a proof of something, as an example, or merely to satisfy the listener's wishes. At the same time he may try to attract attention, to find amusing expressions or to enter into intensive interaction with the listener. Whatever the narrator's goals or intentions, they always effect both the choice of narrative and the mode of performance" (See in Handoo, *et al*, 1999, 137).

Mieke Bal in *Narratology: Introduction to the Theory of Narrative* defines a narrative as containing an actor and a narrator as:

> A narrative text is a text in which an agent relates a narrative. A story is a fabula that is presented in

a certain manner. A fabula is a series of logically
and chronologically related events that are caused or
experienced by actors… (Bal, 1985, 8).

According to Abbott, narrative is the principal way in
which our species organizes its understanding of 'time' and
the ability to manage time 'fluidly' within a narrative allows
"events themselves to create the order of time" (Abbott
2002, 3).

Seymour Chatman's (1978) main contribution to the
theory of narrative is *Story and Discourse*. He explains that
story is the content of narrative 'the what' and the discourse
is form of narrative 'the how'. According to the author the
structuralist theory of narrative states that narrative has two
parts - text and structure. The first part, the story, consists
of the content - the chain of events and the existents -the
characters and the items of setting. The second part, the
discourse, is the means by which the content is expressed
(Chatman, 1978, 478).

Roman Jakobson *On Realism in Art* (1921) argues
that literature does not exist as a separate entity. He and
many other semioticians prefer the view that all texts,
whether spoken or written, are the same except that some
authors encode their texts with distinctive literary qualities
that distinguish them from other forms of discourse.
Nevertheless, there is a clear trend to address literary
narrative forms as separable from other forms. This is
first seen in *Russian* Formalism through Victor Shklovsky's
analysis of the relationship between composition and style,
and through the works of Vladimir Propp who analyzed the
plots used in traditional folktales and identified their distinct
functional components. This trend continues in the work of
the Prague School and of French scholars such as Claude
Levi-Strauss and Roland Barthes. It leads to a structural

analysis of narrative and an increasingly influential body of modern works that raises important epistemological as well as ontological questions: as to how a narrative is manifested as art, in cinema, theatre, or literature and how poetry, short stories and novels are evolved in their respective genres as well as it raises the question as to what a text is? What role does it have in the context of culture?

For general purposes in Semiotics and Literary Theory, a 'narrative' is accepted as a story or part of a story. It may be in spoken, written or in imagined form, and it will have one or more points of view representing some or all the participants or observers. The *A·chiks* like most of the tribal communities have a rich storehouse of oral texts – stories, songs, riddles, etc. but can they essentially be part of literary narrative?

Whatever the form, the content may concern real-world people and events. This is termed personal experience narrative. When the content is fictional, different conventions apply.

Everyday narration and narratives serve important functions in the normal management of everyday life. Encounters with foreign countries and cultural differences, with 'strange habits' and 'alien behaviours', exotic food ways and table manners, incomprehensible norms and values, are such experiences, and we may surmise that for the management of such intercultural experiences, narration and narratives play a significant role: on the individual level, they may function, for example, as parts of intercultural interactions, as stories about strange events that help the narrator accommodate to cultural differences, or as example for teaching others how to interact with strangers or partners from another country. On the collective level, narratives may function as stabilizers of identities or as makers of ethnic or cultural boundaries (Klaus Roth, 118).

According to Klaus Roth, it can be summarized, that narratives play a role in and for intercultural communication in that they are as narrated by (i) representation of a culture, (ii) reveal the image of other cultures, (iii) play a role in the actual communicative acts between people from different cultures, (iv) are used for the communication about culture contacts and conflicts, and (v) play a role in the teaching of intercultural competence (Klaus Roth, 118).

These five ideas are inter-related and interdependent. The narratives differ, however, in two important dimensions: they function either as collective, general narratives or in real intercultural encounters, and they function on different levels of cultural awareness or reflection - from the unreflected telling stories to the skilful and highly reflected use of narratives for ideological, artistic or didactic purposes (Klaus Roth, 119).

1.4.1. Narratives as Expressions or Representations of Cultures

Narratives are 'culture-laden'. Folktales and legends, jests and jokes, proverbs etc are expressions or representations of the culture world view values, customs, institutions and history. The stories thus provide clues for better understanding of people and culture (Klaus Roth, 120).

Narratives can also represent a culture in various other ways. *Volkseele* or the search for the 'soul of the people' in the folk poetry that began in the late 18th century initiated the exercise of collecting and studying of fairy tales, legends, myths, songs and ballads in many countries. This search was linked to nationalism as well. This exercise had nation building, nationalism, and 'invention of traditions' of 'treasury of folklore'. Thus the very exercise of returning to the folk became the integral part of nation building agenda (Klaus Roth, 120).

Folklores are expressions of the culture and reflective of the self image of the community as they even can be seen as the makers of the self image of the community. Tales and legends, and songs were collected, edited and archived because they were perceived as representations (and presentations) of national identity, as poetic expression of the essence of one's own ethnic group or nation, as visible expressions of one's 'national character' (Klaus Roth, 120).

1.4.2. Narratives as Perceptions of Other Cultures

Narratives about other groups or cultures express either the collective historical experience with, or the perception of 'other' cultures, either in negative, hostile terms, or in friendly and positive terms. Experiences of other people can happen through war, colonization, trade, travel, geographical proximity, or multinational or multicultural experience. These knowledge about other cultures as Handoo would call, also define boundaries between groups (Handoo, et al, 1999, 121).

Folktales and legends, riddles and anecdotes, jokes, slurs and mockery about ethnic groups as well as derogatory names and nicknames of other peoples can perpetuate prejudices, hatred and enmities between peoples. They can even jeopardize inter cultural communications. Since they are accepted as cultural expressions they can, on the other hand also mitigate tensions and help to adapt to and get used to cultural differences (Klaus Roth, 121).

Handoo mentions about narratives in culture contact situations, culture contact stories, and critical incidents about didactic tools and narratives crossing cultural boundaries.

1.4.3. Narratives as Units in Cultural Contact Situations

Cultural contact stories are individual or collective narrative renderings of intercultural interactions, usually of surprising, critical, unexpected or unexplainable experiences and conflicts. Cultural contact stories can be viewed as a way of talking about cultural differences or intercultural interactions which help bridging cultural gaps between communities (Klaus Roth, 124).

1.4.4. Culture Contact Stories

The cultural contact stories are marked by tendencies toward episodisation, legendary, and towards traditionalisation. In other words, they tend to focus and elaborate on impressive or extreme or spectacular elements thereby enhancing differences.

1.4.5. 'Critical Incidents' as Didactic Tools

It is the ability to manage cultural diversity, communicate and interact successfully other cultures which is called intercultural competence. The 'critical incidents' are an indispensable didactic tool because they make use of the basic human activity of learning from examples and by imitation (Handoo et al, 1999, 126).

1.4.6. Managing Crossing Cultural Boundaries

Managing diversity is a major issue in our world which tears down borders, creates new multinational states and has established global relations. Cultural contact stories have both the potentialities of greater inter cultural understanding and the vulnerabilities of inter cultural anxieties.

1.5. Functions of Narrative

The basic purpose of narrative is to entertain, to gain and hold a readers' interest. However, narratives can also be written to teach or inform, to change attitudes/social opinions, e.g. soap operas and television dramas that are used to raise topical issues.

Bascom points out that "in non-literate societies … it is important to learn myths and legends because they contain information that is believed to be true" (Bascom, 1972). He observes how in African societies folktales are regarded important for education. Folk narratives have immense educational value in all societies, especially in the ones where tradition is prevalent like in India.

Functions as social authority, social control and cultural continuity are more intimately connected with myths; these are nonetheless brought into play often through other narrative genres like legends and tales. As far back as 1926, Malinowski had emphasized the importance of the myth as sacred stories to social patterns of behavior, to ritual, to religion, and to 'practical guides'. According to Malinowski myths strengthen traditions and endow it with greater values (See Bascom, 1972).

Folklore also functions as an 'escape mechanism', as Handoo points out, "revealing man's frustrations and attempts to escape in fantasy from repressions imposed upon him by society… (and) from the conditions of his geographical environment and also from his biological limitations" have been found to be active through all the narratives of different genres available in different regions and communities of India which, we are sure, can exemplify this intriguing function of folklore most convincingly. The functions of different genres of folklore, including narrative genres, have undergone modifications and transformations of various kinds. In some cases, the functions of particular genres have been suitably adjusted to serve changed situations while in others they have been consciously put to new kinds of use or made to serve new kinds of needs.

Barbara Hardy made a hyperbolic claim for the narrative structure of most of our activities, she writes "We dream in narrative, day dream in narrative, remember, anticipate, hope, despair, believe, doubt, plan, revise, criticize, construct, gossip, learn, hate and love by narrative" (qtd. in Rimmon-Kenan, 2006, 12).

The present study is an attempt to make enquiry of the folk narratives of the *A·chiks*, the functions they have been serving and the greater cultural implications they carry. In terms of the so called developmental or modernizing interventions are concerned, the *A·chik* society has largely remained traditional rather than 'modern', the common *A·chik* folk has retained the century old intimacy with their tribal life-world, have the world of their folk narrative provides critical dues to the cultural hinterland of the community, their belief system, social structure, rituals and their implications, as well as their spiritual and ethical world view.

1.6. Myth

The word 'myth' is derived from the Greek word *muthos* which literally means a tale or something one utters, in a wide range of senses: a statement, a story, the plot of a play. The word 'mythology' in English denotes either the study of myths, or their content, or a particular set of myths. Malinowski differentiates myth from legend and fairytale and so according to him legends were told and believed as if they were history but they do not contain any miraculous or sacred element. Fairytales narrate miraculous happenings but are not in any way linked with ritual, they belong to the realm of entertainment. For him, myth, on the other hand is a statement of a higher and a more important truth, of primeval reality, which is still regarded as the pattern and foundation of primitive life (Malinowski, 1967, 305).

Human beings desire to know and reach the ultimate being and ultimate knowledge. Undoubtedly, with the advent of science and the scientific method, mythology has been rejected as the product of superstitious and primitive minds. Of late there is growing interest in the significance of the nature and role of myth in human life and history. Claude Lévi-Strauss, in his *Myth and Meaning* (1978) profoundly brings to light the insights of myth in order to understand and have much appreciation of `myth in the life of human person and history. Strauss points out that since the birth of knowledge, myth has been an integral part of human life. Besides, he mentions that myths get thought in man 'unbeknownst' to him (1978, 3). Myth describes a lived experience, for it says exactly how one perceives one's own relation to his/her work. Currently, most of the things of the past are already bygone. Levi Strauss emphasizes that now there is a greater realization and so science is making an all out effort to reintegrate them in the field of scientific explanation. Hence, myth and science should go hand in hand in this world (Levi-Strauss, 1978).

1.6.1. Myth and Profane Stories

R. W. Firth found out that it is not easy to separate the sacred stories (myths) from the profane ones. Some tales are sacred clearly and explicitly, for they deal with supernatural beings, powerful spirits, and it is dangerous to tell them in any other than the prescribed way; but at the same time we notice that the same supernatural beings appear also in fairytales or entertainment stories. We can indicate a characteristic by which myths can be distinguished from other tales; sacredness and a close connection with ritual.

Dhavamony (1973) opines that in societies where myths are still alive and meaningful, the people carefully distinguish myths from true stories, fables and false stories. He makes an elaborate observation of myths. The special circumstance in which myths are told or taught brings out again the difference between myths and fables or false stories. Tribal people communicate the knowledge of myths only to the initiated whereas legends and other tales are recited before the uninitiated. Generally the elders during their isolation in the bush communicate the myths to the initiated, which forms part of the initiation ritual. But legends and tales can be recited anywhere and at any time. Both myths and legends narrate histories, i.e., a series of events that took place in a distant and fabulous past. But the actors in the myths are generally gods and supernatural beings; actors in the legends and tales are heroes or miraculous animals. Though the contents of both types of stories, myths and legends, are of the everyday world, myths are considered to affect the people directly and to have altered the human condition as such, while legends and tales have not altered, the human condition as such, although they have caused changes in the world in a limited way (1973, 139).

Myths narrate how one's state of affairs became another; how an unpeopled world became populated; how chaos became cosmos; how immortals became mortal; how the seasons came to replace a climate without seasons; how the original unity of mankind became a plurality of tribes or nations and so on. Myths, in brief, tell us not only about the origin of the world, of animals, of plants and of man but also the primordial events as a result of which man finds himself in a situation such as he finds himself in at the present time, mortal, sexed, organized in society, forced to work and to live according to a set of norms. Besides the cosmogony and anthropogenic, other events belonging to mythical times occurred, on account of which man is affected and becomes what he is today. Namely, if a certain tribe lives on fishing it is because in mythical times a supernatural being taught its ancestors to catch and cook fish (see Dhavamony, 1973, 139).

For the primitive man myths are of primary importance. By living the myths by means of the rituals, the religious man is able to imitate and reproduce the divine beings and their activities, to commune with the divine by symbolically participating in the original state of beings as created and ordained by the divine and supernatural beings. To know the myths is to learn the secret of the origin of things, to enter into living relation with the origin of things, to be able to reproduce the original order of things when they gradually degenerate or to make it reappear when they disappear (Eliade, 1969, vol.15, 1134-35).

1.6.2. Reality of Myths

The reality of myths is explained differently by different authors. Social anthropologist, Malinowski holds that myth as it exists in a savage society is not merely a story told but a reality lived. It is an active force in the life of the primitives. By reality of the myths, Malinowski intended to say that myths are charters of extant social institutions (see Dhavamony, 1973, 142). For Gustav Carl Jung, the primitive society does not invent myths but experiences them (142). For Mircea Eliade, myths are always recitals of creations; they tell how something was accomplished, began to *be* (Mircea Eliade, 1959, 95). Hence, myths imply the ontology and speak only of realities; namely what really happened. Eliade means by 'reality' of the myth the sacred reality, the sacred which alone is pre-eminently real; the sacred presents itself as something wholly other than the real, really real, saturated with being, endowed with power. It is a sacred history; hence to relate it means to reveal a mystery. The sacred realm is revealed in the myths; but for the myths they are inaccessible to us (Turner, 577-78).

Myth and ritual recreate in profane time what is true eternally in the sacred reality. To live in the myth is to live out the creative power that is the foundation of existence. Myths cannot be reduced to giving information about something even about the divine beings or primordial events. Myths reveal the sacred and manifest its power. Man by reciting the myth not only learns something but becomes something. In other words, myths by being told manifest sacred power. Hence, we understand why myths are treated so sacredly, guarded so secretly, recited so solemnly, only in ritual and only by the initiands or by the initiated.

Myths and legends are traditional verbal materials passed on orally rather than in written form through generations. They form an essential part of the *A·chiks*. The *A·chiks* have developed a rich store of folklore; not the least among numerous myths is those connected with rivers and the physical features of the lands they settled in. Archetypes occur in different times and places in myth, literature, folklore and rituals. Myths make a larger part of the thematic content of their oral narratives and poetry. Myths serve to explain the intentions and actions of supernatural beings. Most myths are concerned with religion, which involve rituals and prescribed forms of sacred ceremonies. Some of the recurring myths that have strong presence in the cultured narratives of the *A·chiks* are associated with *Balpakram*, the rivers, the spirits, the mountains, the ideas of reincarnations, the whirlpools etc

The *A·chiks* who practice the traditional religion are very religious and god-fearing people. They believe that all physical ailments, accidents and unnatural deaths are due to the wrath of one or the other malevolent spirits. Therefore, sacrifices of animals and birds must be offered to the deities to appease them as well as to invoke their blessings (Milton Sangma, 1981, 233). Myths have got existential functions for man. The indispensable function which myth fulfills in primitive culture is to express, enhance and codify belief, to safeguard and enforce morality to vouch for the efficiency of the ritual and to contain practical rules for the guidance of man. Thus myth is a force that helps to maintain society itself. Myth and religion as a whole continue to play an important part in social life. Myths do not reflect the totality of social structure as myth is always selective but myths do convey a certain meaning for the religious man, besides providing a charter for social action and religious belief.

In indigenous *A·chik* religion too myths play an important role. The function of myths is neither explanatory nor symbolic. It is a statement of an extraordinary event, the occurrence of which had once and for all established the social order of a tribe or some of its economic pursuits, its arts and crafts, of its religious or magical beliefs and ceremonies.

It is the traditional handing down of stories and folk songs, of riddles and puzzles, of dramatic games and dances, depicting their failure and success, the importance of religion and magic, of totems and taboos, or of disciplines and customs, the roles or work and games, of hunger and work, of tribal sentiments and aspirations from generation to generation.

Myths preserve the past of the communities, record the rise and fall of kingdoms and serve as a significant storehouse of community history. It reflects people and also brings in solidarity, continuity and consistency in a cultural group. Myths definitely help in preserving cultures and religion.

Chapter II

Understanding Myths and Archetypes

2.1. Meanings of Myth

The word *mythology* comes from the Greek *mythología*, meaning 'a story-telling, a legendary lore'. It is derived from the word *mythos* meaning narrative, speech, word, fact, and story, *logos* meaning speech, oration, discourse, quote, study, reason and argument. In *Some Meanings of Myth* (1959), Harry Levin explains the original meaning of the word as a 'word' which means *mythos*. With the suffix logos one gets the word 'mythology'. Thus, in a certain sense, the science of myth also means 'the word or words', which should be a caveat against excessive verbiage. An exploded example is the hypothesis of Max Muller that all myths were originally derived from words through a species of allegorical etymology. (1959, 223) *Mythos* is used for 'word' or 'speech' in Homer and in other Greek poets, as differentiated from *logos* that is 'tale' or 'story' (1959, 224).

The term mythology has been in use since at least the last 15th century, which means 'the study or exposition of myths'. The additional meaning of 'body of myths' itself dates back to 1781. In extended use, the word can also refer to collective or personal ideological or socially constructed received wisdom. The mythical belief dates back to 1678. The historical approach was set forth in 1725 by the monumental treatise of Giambattista Vico's, *Principi di una Scienza Nuova intorno alla Natura della Nazioni*. Vico proposed that mythology be read as proto history. He discerned in myth not only the outlines of his spiral theory of progress, but a key to the so called Homeric problem and a working model for the development of law(1959, 226).

Myth, in general use, is often interchangeable with legend or allegory, but some scholars strictly distinguish the terms. The term has been used in English since the 19th century. Myths are Cosmogonic Narratives, connected with the Foundation or Origin of the Universe, though often specifically in terms of a particular culture or region. Given the connection to origins, the setting is typically primordial and characters are proto-human or deific. Myths also often have cosmogonic overtones even when not fully cosmogonic, for instance the myth relating to the origins of important elements of culture like food, medicine, ceremonies, etc.

By contrast, legends are stories about the past, which generally include, or are based on some historical events; generally focused on human heroes and folktales/fairytales or *Märchen* (the German word for such tales). Legends are stories which lack any definite historical setting and often include such things as fairies, witches, a fairy guide and animal characters.

Myths are Narratives of a Sacred Nature, often connected with some ritual. Myths are often foundational. They are key narratives associated with religions as well. A myth is a narrative of events. It has a sacred quality and the sacred communication is made in symbolic form. At least some of the events and objects which occur in the myth actually neither occur nor exist in the world other than in the myth itself. The narrative quality distinguishes a myth from a general idea or a set of ideas, such as a cosmology. The sacred quality and the reference to origins and transformations distinguish myth from legend and other types of folk-tales. Campbell in *The Power of Myth* (1991) says, "A ritual is the enactment of a myth. By participating in a ritual, you are participating in a myth" (1991, 103). Within any given culture there may be sacred and secular myths coexisting. In his article, *The Necessity of Myth* (1959), Mark Schorer quotes Maslinowski who says that myth continually modified and renewed by the modifications of history, is in some form an "indispensable ingredient of all cultures" (1959, 361- 62).

From the earlier work of Malinowski on myth we see the intimate relation of myths as sacred stories to social patterns of behaviour, to ritual, to religion and to practical ethics. His is a sociological theory, according to which myth performs an indispensable function in primitive societies.

Ihab Hassan writes that myth performs in primitive societies an indispensable function: it expresses, enhances and codifies belief. It enforces morality, vouches for the efficiency of ritual and contains practical rules for the guidance of man. So "myth is not poetic, not symbolic, and not explanatory, it is faith and emotion channeled to specific cultural purposes" (1952, 206-207).

According to William G. Doty, myths are narratives which are formative or reflective of social order or values within a culture. Myths are narratives representative of a particular epistemology or way of understanding nature and organizing thought. Myths are the narrative fictions whose plots are read first at the level of their own stories, and then as projections of imminent transcendent meanings.

Such plots mirror human potentialities, experiences with natural and cultural phenomena, and recognition of regular interactions between them. Myths, thus provide possible materializations for otherwise inchoate or unrecognized instantiations (1980, 538).

In *A Comprehensive Definition of Myth* (1980) Doty further confirms that, myths may mean differently at different stages of our lives (535). It may be regarded as a personal or a tribal possession, to be shared as a gift, and may be considered as a form of real property. Myths are the primary stories of a culture, that shape and expose its most important framing images and self-conceptions and its 'roots' (1980, 543).

Mythic narratives often involve heroic characters, possibly proto-humans, super humans, or gods who mediate inherent, troubling dualities, and reconcile us to our realities, or establish the patterns for life as we know it. A structuralist anthropologist, Claude Levi-Strauss, saw myths as stemming from a human need to make sense of the world and to resolve cultural dilemmas. These dilemmas are embodied in the structure of myths, which is made up of opposites, such as good-bad, night-day, etc. For Levi-Strauss, myths are a kind of universal language. While the events of myths vary, the basic structures, like grammar, are similar in myths worldwide because people are similar. On another level of 'making sense', myths explain the world, making it manageable. For example, the myths worldwide in which human beings are fashioned from clay by a divine potter, such as the Egyptian Ptah, fulfils our need to know how and why we came to be here. In *The Structural Study of Myth* (1955) Strauss says:

> Myths are still widely interpreted in conflicting ways: collective dreams, the outcome of a kind of aesthetics play, the foundation of ritual …Mythological figures

are considered as personified abstractions, divinized heroes or decayed gods. Whatever the hypothesis, the choice amounts to reducing mythology either to an idle play or to a coarse kind of speculation (1955, 428).

He further states that myths are narratives that are 'Counter-Factual in featuring actors and actions that confound the conventions of routine experience.' Some claim that human societies merely express, through their mythology, fundamental feelings common to the whole of humankind, such as love, hate, revenge; or that they try to provide some kind of explanations for phenomena which they cannot understand otherwise: astronomical, meteorological, and the like. On the other hand, psychoanalysts and many anthropologists have shifted the problems to be explained away from the natural or cosmological fields to the sociological and psychological fields (1955, 428-429).

Northrop Frye, on the other hand, identifies myth with literature asserting that myth is a 'structural organizing principle of literary form' and that an archetype is essentially an element of one's literary experiences (Geurin, *et al*, 1999, 166). In its archetypal aspect art is a part of civilization, whose major concerns, as it develops, are the city, the gardens, the farm, the sheepfold and human society. Therefore, an archetypal symbol is usually associated with a natural object with human meaning, and it forms part of the critical view of art as a civilized product, a vision of the goals of human work.

The word 'myth' means different things in different fields, opines Robert Denham in *Northrop Frye on Culture and Literature* (1978). In literary criticism, it is gradually settling down to mean the formal or constructive principle of literature. In anonymous stories about gods they become legends and are part of folk tales in later ages; then they gradually become more 'realistic', that is, adapted to a popular demand for plausibility, though they retain the same structural outlines. Profound or classic works of art are frequently, almost regularly, marked by a tendency to revert or allude to the archaic and explicit form of the myth in the god-story. When there is no story, or when a theme (Aristotle's 'dianoia') is the centre of the action instead of a 'mythos', the formal principle is a charged idea or sense data. Myths in this sense are readily translatable: they are, in fact, the communicable ideogrammatic structures of literature (Denham 1978, 74).

The myth of concern comprises everything that a society is most concerned to know. It is the disposition which leads man to uphold communal, rather than individual values. Frye says:

> A myth of concern has its roots in religion and only later branches out into politics, law and literature. It is inherently traditional and conservative, placing a strong emphasis on values of coherence and continuity. It originates in oral or preliterate culture and is associated with continuous verse conventions and discontinuous prose forms. And it is "deeply attached to ritual, to coronations, weddings, funerals, parades, demonstrations, where something is publicly done that expresses an inner social identity" (Denham, 1978, 14).

According to C. G. Jung and C. Kerenyi, myths are original revelations of the preconscious psyche, involuntary statements about unconscious psychic happenings and anything but allegories of physical processes. Myths have a vital meaning:

> They are the psychic life of the primitive tribe, which immediately falls to pieces and decays when it loses its mythological heritage, like a man who has lost his soul (Jung, *et al*, 1978, 73).

Myths are the symbolic projections of people's hopes, values, fears and aspirations (Guerin *et al*, 1999, 159). They are merely primitive fictions, illusions, or opinions based upon false reasoning according to the common misconceptions and misuse of the terms. Myth is, in the general sense, universal. As Guerin points it "myths are by nature collective and communal, they bind a tribe or a nation together in common psychological and spiritual activities. It is the expression of a profound sense of togetherness of feeling and of action and of wholeness of living" (1999, 160). Myth and dream are the outside and inside of the human unconscious. Together they form the realm of the archetypes. And as myth is a codification of our unconscious archetypes, literature is the cultural realization of our mythologies. Myths and stories from our past have been used, interpreted, and reinterpreted for hundreds of years to create new stories. Through this process a number of 'archetypes' have been created. Myths are metaphorical representations of the content of the archetypes and used to provide us with information about life's experiences.

According to Jung, "myths are the means by which archetypes, essentially unconscious forms, become manifest and articulate to the conscious mind." Jung indicated further that archetypes reveal themselves in the dreams of individuals, so that we might say that dreams are 'personalized myths' and myths are 'depersonalized dreams' (1999, 179).

Myths are the instruments by which we continually struggle to make our experience intelligible to ourselves opine Mark Schorer, in *The Necessity of Myth*:

> A myth is a large, controlling image that gives philosophical meaning to the facts of ordinary life; that is, which has organizing value for experience. A mythology is a more or less articulated body of such images, a pantheon. Without such images, experience is chaotic, fragmentary and merely phenomenal (1959, 360).

He further says that myth is fundamental, the dramatic representation of our deepest instinctual life, of a primary awareness of man in the universe, capable of many configurations, upon which all particular opinions and attitudes depend (1959, 361).

In *The Meanings of 'Myth' in Modern Criticism* (1953) Wallace Douglas says that "a society that possesses myths is a healthy human society… (But myths) will come into being, as they probably have in the past, only out of deep and long-continued passion, crystallized and given shape, perhaps, by some deeply passionate seer-artist, and slowly absorbed into a common culture because they reflect or create profound convictions and satisfy the impossible ideas of that culture" (234).

Douglas points out that the mythic involves insights into the universal or commerce between the community and the mysteries, and undertakes a part of the ordering of experience. Myth deals with the 'fundamentals of our existence', it is derived from 'the word as the most ancient, the original account of the origins of the world;' it also imbeds a 'complex of human problems' or carries 'one of the archetypes from the collective unconscious of mankind' or 'the timeless meaning' of an individual's psychic life. In what must be its widest senses, 'myth in its union with logos, comprises the totality of human existence,' or, as 'the myth', it is 'the totality of all visions of truth which are untestable, non-demonstrable, non-empirical, and non-logical' (1953, 236).

He further quotes Nietzsche, who assumes that a modern man is essentially different in his modes of thinking and feeling from primitive man: he is so broken up by the critico-historical spirit of our culture, that he can only make the former existence of myth credible to himself by learned means through intermediary abstractions. Without myth, any culture would lose its healthy creative power. Myth gives meaning to the foundations of the state and to the life of the individual (1953, 238-39).

Reviews of myths, legends, fairy tales, epic poems, novels and films reveal that the protagonist types who recur in these stories fall into sixteen distinctive categories, eight each for the heroes and heroines. At his or her core every well-defined hero or heroine is one of the respective archetypes. The archetype tells the writer about the most basic instincts of the hero: how he thinks, feels, what drives him and why he chooses both his goals and his methods. The skilful writer, in turn, conveys these instincts to the readers or audience, who, knowing at a glance the character of this hero, settles down to watch the tale retold anew.

In the *Language of Poetry*, Philip Wheelwright explains, "myth is the expression of a profound sense of togetherness of feeling and of action and of wholeness of living" (Guerin, *et al*, 1999, 160). For Alan W. Watts, "myth is to be defined as a complex of stories, some no doubt fact, and some fantasy which for various reasons, human beings regard as demonstrations of the inner meaning of the universe and of human life" (1999, 160).

Eugene Ionesco says that there is nothing truer than myth: history, in its attempt to realize myth, distorts it, stops halfway; when history claims to have succeeded, this is nothing but humbug and mystification. Everything we dream is realizable. Reality does not have to be: it is simply what it is. Robert Graves said of Greek myth: "True myth may be defined as the reduction to narrative shorthand of ritual mime performed on public festivals, and in many cases recorded pictorially" (en.wikipedia. org/wiki/mythology-20/8/08). Moreover, myths or extended narratives are often acted out in dramatic rituals. As such, myths become the scripts for the dramas of rituals, and rituals are performances and interpretations of myths (Power, 1986, 451).

Graves was deeply influenced by Sir James George Frazer's mythography, *The Golden Bough*[4] *(1922),* and he would

---

[4]   The *Golden Bough* is a study of unconscious social symbolism as expressed in rituals and hence it is closely linked, as Freud immediately recognised, to Psychology, which studies unconscious individual symbolism of the unconscious as expressed in dreams. At the heart of the animistic symbolism is the theme of death and rebirth. The theme that is studies in The Golden Bough in terms of social ritual and in Jung's Symbols of Transformation and elsewhere in terms of individual dream (Frye, 1978, 100-01). The Golden Bough identifies shared practices and mythological beliefs between primitive religions and modern religions. He argues that the death-rebirth myth is present in almost all cultural mythologies, and is acted out in terms of growing seasons and vegetation. The myth is

have agreed that myths are generated by many cultural needs. Myths authorize the cultural institutions of a tribe, a city, or a nation by connecting them with universal truths. Myths justify the current occupation of a territory by a people, for instance. All cultures have developed over time their own myths, consisting of narratives of their history, their religions, and their heroes. The great power of the symbolic meaning of these stories for the culture is a major reason why they survive as long as they do, sometimes for thousands of years.

Myths are often linked to the spiritual or religious life of a community, and endorsed by rulers or priests. Once this link to the spiritual leadership of society is broken, they often acquire traits that are characteristic of fairy tales. In folkloristic, which is concerned with the study of both secular and sacred narratives, a myth also derives some of its power from being more than a simple 'tale', by comprising an archetypical quality of 'truth'.

Myths are often intended to explain the universal and local beginnings like 'creation myths' and 'founding myths', natural phenomena, otherwise inexplicable cultural conventions or rituals, and anything else for which no simple explanation presents itself. Myth is not merely a story told, but a reality lived, a sanction for a way of life and a pattern for worship. The myth is simply the word itself, and it possesses divine power by its repetition.

Myths never remain static, as they are continually retold and re-written; and in this process they are modulated and transformed. Peter Munz in *History and Myth* (1956) elaborates this idea thus:

---

symbolized by the death (i.e. final harvest) and rebirth (i.e. spring) of the god of vegetation.

The myth which is thus distilled from or composed out of the original historical events can again be described as a concrete universal. It is a concrete story about certain people with definite names and about certain events in definite places. But it is a universal story in that it portrays the most universal patterns of human life, such as motherhood, fatherhood, elemental envy or devotion (1956, 8).

MacIver, in *Acculturation and Myth* (1973) opines "by myths we mean the value-impregnated beliefs and notions that men hold, that they live by or live for." Every society is held together by a myth-system, a complex of dominating thought-forms that determines and sustains all its activities. All social relations, the very texture of human society, are myth-born and myth-sustained. It is through its myths that a society is able to trace its identity. It is through its myths that a social group is able to distinguish itself from other groups (Signorile, 1973, 119).

In *Myth, Memory, and the Oral Tradition* (1976) Frances Harwood says that an intimate connection exists between the world, the 'mythos', the sacred tales of a tribe, on the one hand, and their ritual acts, their moral deeds, their social organization, and even their practical activities on the other (1976, 784).

Bronislaw Malinowski justifies that myth fulfils in primitive cultures an indispensable function: it expresses, enhances and codifies belief; it safeguards and enforces morality; it vouches for the efficacy of ritual and contains practical rules for the guidance of man. Myth is thus a vital ingredient of human civilization; it is not an ideal tale, but an active force; it is not an intellectual explanation or an artistic imagery, but a pragmatic charter of primitive faith and moral wisdom (1976, 785). For him myths are viewed as charters for social institutions. This formulation turns on two concepts – that of myth as a charter and that of an institution as an ethnographic category.

The similar view is highlighted by Jung *In Essays on a Science of Mythology*, (1993). He says thus:

> The myth in a primitive society, i.e., in its original living form, is not a mere tale told but a reality lived. It is not in the nature of an invention such as we read in our novels today, but living reality, believed to have occurred in primordial times and to be influencing ever afterwards the world and the destinies of men… These stories are kept alive by vain curiosity, neither as tales that have been invented nor again as tales that are true. For the natives on the contrary they are the assertion of an original, greater, and more important reality through which the present life, fate, and work of mankind are governed, and the knowledge of which provides men on the one hand with motives for ritual and moral acts, on the other with direction for their performance (1993, 5).

2.2. Functions of Myth

Campbell in *The Power of Myth* (1991) identifies four functions of myth. According to him the first is the mythical function which makes one to realize the great mysteries of the universe, the human beings. Myth opens the world to the dimension of mystery, to the realization of the mystery that underlies all forms. The second is a cosmological dimension; the dimension with which science is concerned shows the shape of the universe. The third function is the sociological one supporting and validating a certain social order (Campbell, *et al*, 1991, 38-39) and the fourth function is pedagogical that is how to live a human lifetime under any circumstance (Campbell, *et al*, 1991, 87).

Percy S. Cohen, in *Theories of Myth* (1969) quotes Levi-Strauss who says that the main function of myth, the main cause promoting its existence as a mode of thought, is that it is a device for 'mediating contradictions' or 'oppositions' as experienced by men. According to him all myth performs a number of functions simultaneously. For whatever reasons myths were originally invented, they were subsequently used as a vehicle for communicating or just expressing a number of things for which they may never have been intended. Let us say that myths were originally explanations of the origins or transformations of things or, as I would prefer to put it, let us say that they were originally devices for blocking off explanation (1969, 351).

Handoo in *Folklore in Modern India* (1998) considers the functions of myth as social authority, social control and cultural continuity as enumerated by Bascom.

Myths are not the same as fables, legends, folktales, fairytales, anecdotes or fiction, but the concepts may overlap. Notably, during Romanticism, famously by the Brothers Grimm and Elias Lonnrot, folktales and fairytales were perceived as eroded fragments of earlier mythology. Mythological themes are also very often consciously employed in literature, beginning with Homer.

Comparative mythology is the systematic comparison of myths from different cultures. It seeks to discover underlying themes that are common to the myths of multiple cultures. In some cases, comparative mythologists use the similarities between different mythologies to argue that those mythologies have a common source. This common source may be a common source of inspiration or a common 'proto mythology' that diverged into the various mythologies. Nineteenth century interpretations of myth were often highly comparative. However, modern day scholars tend to be more suspicious of comparative approaches, avoiding overly general or universal statements about mythology.

In a scholarly setting, the word 'myth' may mean 'sacred story', 'traditional story', or 'story involving gods', but it does not mean 'false story'. Therefore, many scholars refer to a religion's stories as 'myths' without intending to offend members of that religion. Religion begins with a sense of wonder and awe and the attempt to tell stories that will connect us to God. Then it becomes a set of theological works in which everything is reduced to a code, to a creed. Religion turns poetry to prose (Campbell, *et al*, 1991, 173-74). Nevertheless, this scholarly use of the word 'myth' may cause misunderstanding and offend people who cherish those myths. This is because word 'myth' is popularly used to mean 'falsehood'. Many myths, such as ritual myths, are clearly part of religion. However, unless we simply define myths as 'sacred stories', not all myths are necessarily religious.

Harry M. Buck makes a brilliant analysis. According to him, myths that are based on a historical event over time become imbued with symbolic meaning, transformed, shifted in time or place, or even reversed. One way of conceptualizing this process is to view 'myths' as lying at the far end of a continuum ranging from a 'dispassionate account' to 'legendary occurrence' to 'mythical status'. As an event progresses towards the mythical end of this continuum, what people think, feel and say about the event takes on progressively greater historical significance while the facts become less important by the time one reaches the mythical end of the story. "Myth is not merely a story told, but a reality lived, a sanction for a way of life and a pattern for worship. The myth is simply the word itself, and it possesses divine power by its repetition" (1961, 220). The narration of events and reference to objects unknown outside the world differentiates myth from history or Pseudo history.

Myth, as mentioned earlier, has a history and a development. The old theory of euhemerism is an attempt to understand the genesis of myth. It is now generally accepted that the folktale preceded mythology in human history (Ihab H. Hassan, 1952, 213).

Myth is a fascinating and many-facetted subject. There are myths, sagas, and fairytales; there is folklore and superstition. There are ancient myths, modern myths, or urban myths, that supposedly have taken place in our own time. Collectively all of this can be labeled 'traditions'.

The purpose of science is to find the truth, in a literal, physical sense. The role of fiction is to entertain. They have variously been interpreted as distorted history, as remnants from an obsolete religion, and as entertainment. There are several more paradigms as how to interpret myth. Sigmund Freud, for instance, might have interpreted the roll as a manifestation of sexuality, while Jung might have sought the image of the roll in the common subconscious. Robert Graves often interpreted Greek myths as misunderstood symbols from an earlier religion. His Irish background with its own rich mythology may well have guided his interpretations, but if that is for the better or worse can be debated.

Claude Levi-Strauss says that modern Science is not at all moving away from these things, but it is attempting more to reintegrate them in the field of scientific explanation. At that time, with Bacon, Descartes, Newton, and the others, it was necessary for science to build itself up against the old generations of mythical and mystical thought, and it was thought that science could only exist by turning its back upon the world of the senses, the world we see, smell, taste, and perceive; the sensory was a delusive world, whereas the real world was a world of mathematical properties which could only be grasped by the intellect and which was entirely at odds with the false testimony of the senses. The contemporary science is tending to overcome this gap and that more and more the sense data are being reintegrated into scientific explanation as something which has a meaning, a truth, and which can be explained (1978, 5-6).

Mircea Eliade, a philosopher in his appendix to *Myths, Dreams and Mysteries* (1967) and in *The Myth of the Eternal Return* (2005), assumed the existence of 'the sacred' as the object of religious worship, and saw myth as a physical revelation of the sacred. If the sacred interacts with our physical reality it can, at least in principle, be measured and determined to be either true or false. But if it does not interact, it can neither be falsified nor confirmed. However, if it does interact then it is perfectly natural. Thus, if God exists he is a natural phenomenon that has turned first into a myth, and then into religion, it would seem.

Science can make an historic myth intelligible again. On the contrary, they will find that their religion kept the myth alive, so that we today could regain knowledge that would otherwise have been lost forever. Science is then just the process to undo the damage so to say, and mythology has been the vehicle for saving the knowledge.

In *History and Myth*, Peter Munz says that in common usage the two words 'myth' and 'history' are used as if they denoted contradictories. Historians are inclined to call the version of an event which they consider untrue, a myth.

Myth and history, in a very special sense, are interdependent. They fertilize each other; and it is doubtful whether the one could exist without the other (1956, 1).

He further states that one needs to make it clear at the outset that both the naïve conception of myth and history as contradictories and the more subtle notion of their mutual interdependence, are due to the fact that myth and history are stories of concrete events, said to have taken place at a certain time and to have involved certain people. Both kinds of stories differ fundamentally from such general propositions as 'all men are mortal' or, 'unless babies are weaned at a certain moment they are likely to get a mother fixation' (1956, 1-2).

A myth, however, differs qualitatively from a historical account, in that it is vague in its specifications of time and space. But this is not necessarily so, for there are many myths that are by no means vague. A myth is a story of concrete events involving concrete persons. But it is lacking in any precise indication as to the time and place the events happened. We may conclude therefore that the myth, although a story of a concrete event, is not a story of any particular historical event. We can nevertheless speak of a true myth. A true myth is one that draws our attention to a more or less universally valid story. A myth, then, is a true story not because it relates to a particular historical event; but because it exhibits universally true features. And since it is a concrete story, one can call a myth a concrete universal. William L Power, in *Myth, Truth and Justification in Religion* (1986) justifies this:

> Thus, a myth represents reality, if it truly does represent reality, by means of analogies and holistically so, and the truth value of a myth is determined by the same canons of assessment found

in critical inquiry; only those canons are implicit rather than explicit (1986, 456).

We may conclude therefore again that the formation of myth is subject to certain laws and not due to an arbitrary exercise of the imagination. When history is telescoped into myth, the myth-maker always has the objective of bringing out certain features deeply characteristic of human behaviour. The myth-maker feels free to select his/her facts from a wide sphere; he/she is not concerned with the literal truth of his/her story; but with linking facts chosen from a vast field of events into a significant whole, a concrete universal story.

We see, therefore, that the myth which is thus distilled from or composed out of the original historical events can again be described as a concrete universal. It is a concrete story about certain people with definite names and about certain events in definite places. But it is a universal story in that it portrays the most universal patterns of human life, such as motherhood, fatherhood, elemental envy or devotion.

2.3. Theories of Myth

There are many theories of myth, but they are not necessarily rival theories. According to Pre-modern theories, storytellers repeatedly elaborated upon historical accounts until the figures in those accounts gained the status of gods. This theory is named 'euhemerism' after the novelist *Euhemerus* (320 BC) who suggested that the Greek gods were developed from legends about human beings. This theory claims that myths are distorted accounts of real historical events. According to this theory, storytellers repeatedly elaborated upon historical accounts until the figures in those accounts gained the status of gods. It refers to the process of rationalization of myths, putting themes formerly imbued with mythological qualities into pragmatic contexts, for example following a cultural or religious paradigm shift (Jung, 1968, 60).

Some theories propose that myths began as allegories. Apollo represents fire; Poseidon represents water, and so on. According to another theory, myths began as allegories for philosophical or spiritual concepts: Athena represents wise judgment, Aphrodite represents desire, etc. In the 19th century Max Muller supported an allegorical theory of myth. He believed that myths began as allegorical descriptions of nature, but gradually came to be interpreted literally: for example, a poetic description of the sea as 'raging' was eventually taken literally, and the sea was then thought of as a raging god.

Similarly, myths are also resulted from the personification of inanimate objects and forces. According to these thinkers, the ancients worshipped natural phenomena such as fire and air, gradually coming to describe them as gods. According to Jung 'the Deity appears in the garb of Nature' (Jung, 1968, 118).

According to the 'myth-ritual theory', the existence of myth is tied to ritual. In its most extreme form, this theory claims that myths arose to explain rituals. This claim was first put forward by the biblical scholar William Robertson Smith. According to Smith, people begin performing rituals for some reason that is not related to myth; later, after they had forgotten the original reason for a ritual, they tried to account for the ritual by inventing a myth and claiming that the ritual commemorates the events described in that myth. The anthropologist, James Frazer, had a similar theory.

The first scholarly theories of myth appeared during the second half of the 19th century. In general, these 19th century theories framed myth as a failed or obsolete mode of thought, often by interpreting myth as the primitive counterpart of modern science.

For example, E. B. Tylor interpreted myth as an attempt at a literal explanation for natural phenomena in which early man tried to explain natural phenomena by attributing souls to inanimate objects, giving rise to animism. Max Muller called myth a 'disease of language'. The anthropologist James Frazer saw myths as a misinterpretation of magical rituals, which were themselves based on a mistaken idea of natural law.

Many 20th century theories of myth rejected the 19th century theories' opposition of myth and science. In general, 20th century theories have tended to see myth as almost anything but an outdated counterpart to science; consequently, moderns are not obliged to abandon myth for science.

Swiss psychologist Carl Jung (1873-1961) and his followers also tried to understand the psychology behind world myths. Jung argued that the gods of mythology are not material beings, but archetypes or mental states and moods that all humans can feel, share, and experience. He and his adherents believe archetypes directly affect our subconscious perceptions and way of understanding. Following Jung, Joseph Campbell believed that insights about one's psychology, gained from reading myths, can be beneficially applied to one's own life.

Like the psychoanalysts, Claude Levi-Strauss believed that myths reflect patterns in the mind. However, he saw those patterns more as fixed mental structures specifically, pairs of oppositions than as unconscious feelings or urges.

According to Percy S. Cohen, a major critic, there are several types of theory of myth which treats myth as a form of explanation. Sir Edward Burnett Taylor also treats myths as explanation, but considers that they are peculiar explanations; for him, the chief peculiarities are that myths make use of the language of metaphor and that metaphor is used by primitive man to personalize the forces of the natural world which he seeks to understand and control.

Cohen opines that the chief weaknesses of these theories are that they do not explain why myth is social in character, and why the possession of certain myths is not only collective but is significant in marking the identity of a particular social group; and they provide poor accounts of the symbolic content of myth. He also points out that the chief merit of the intellectualist doctrine is that it does recognize that men, including savages, have intellect and, moreover, that they might also have intellectual curiosity (Percy S. Cohen, 1969, 339).

He further illustrates that the Freudian theorists seek to explain, not only why myths take the form they do, but what the source of mythical expression is. In this view, myths are like daydreams which occur in full sleep involving a process known as the dream-work, of symbolically reconstructing messages which emit from the unconscious. In this process two main things occur: the message is disguised; and the body of messages is condensed (1969, 340-41).

Since myth is a type of daydream it makes use of the symbolism of dreams, expressing unconscious wishes and conflicts. But since it is only a daydream the conscious element is strong, it is more readily communicable than a dream (1969, 341).

For Durkheim, myth is part of the religious system, and expresses in words what ritual expresses in actions:

both have a social function of maintaining and expressing solidarity. The content of the myth, in the first place represents certain values which are embodied in social life; secondly, it reflects certain features of social structure. He also points out that myth, along with other religious beliefs, provides the basis of all cultural means of categorizing the world: and this forms the basis of philosophy and science (1969, 343).

Since the beginning of modern philosophy and science in the 16th century, many Western intellectuals have seen myth as outdated. In fact, some argued that the Christian religion would be better off without mythology, or even that Christianity would be better off without religion.

In the 20th century, many scholars have resisted this trend, defending myth from modern criticism. Mircea Eliade, the religious scholar, declared that myth did not hold religion back, that myth was an essential foundation of religion, and that eliminating myth would eliminate a piece of the human psyche. Eliade approached myth sympathetically at a time when religious thinkers were trying to purge religion of its mythological elements.

Similarly, Joseph Campbell believed that people could not understand their individual lives without mythology to aid them. By recalling the significance of old myths, he encouraged awareness of them and the creation of myths for the contemporary age.

Although there is no specific universal myth, there are many themes and motifs that recur in the myths of various cultures and ages. Some cultures have myths of the creation of the world; these range from a god fashioning the earth from abstract chaos to a specific animal creating it from a handful of mud. Other myths of cyclical destruction and creation are paralleled by myths of seasonal death and rebirth. Certain other cultures were concerned with longer periods of vegetative death through prolonged drought. The flood motif is extremely widespread and is one element of a group of myths that concern the destruction and recreation of the world or a particular society. Myths treating the origin of fire, or its retrieval from some being who has stolen it or refused to share it; the millennium to come; and the dead or the relation between the living and the dead, are common.

There have been many theories as to the reasons for similarities among myths. Many have viewed myths merely as poor versions of history, and have attempted to analyze and explicate them in non sacred ways to account for their apparent absurdity. Some ancient Greeks explained myths as allegories, and looked for a reality concealed in poetic images. Another interpretation sees myths as developing from an improper separation between the human and non-human; animals, rocks, and stars are considered to be on a level of intelligence with people, and the dead are thought to inhabit the world of the living in spiritual form.

2.4. Archetypes

Archetypes are elementary ideas, what could be called 'ground' ideas (Campbell, *et al*, 1991, 60). These ideas Jung spoke of as archetype of the unconscious. Archetype of the unconscious means it comes from below and is biologically grounded. The word 'archetype' is derived from the Greek term 'archetypos'. 'Arche' meaning the original, and 'typos' meaning form or model. Thus the term denotes 'original model'. Jung called the recurring personalities as archetypes. It also means the first of its kind.

The origins of the archetypal hypothesis date back as far as to Plato. Jung himself compared archetypes to Platonic ideas. Plato's ideas were pure mental forms that were imprinted in the soul before it was born into the world. They were collective in the sense that they embodied the fundamental characteristics of a thing rather than its specific peculiarities. In fact many of Jung's ideas were prevalent in Athenian philosophy. The archetype theory can be seen as a psychological equivalent to the philosophical idea of forms and particulars.

Archetypes form a dynamic substratum common to all humanity, upon the foundation of which each individual builds his/her own experience of life, developing a unique array of psychological characteristics. Thus, while archetypes themselves may be conceived as innate nebulous forms, from these may arise innumerable images, symbols and patterns of behaviour. While the emerging images and forms are apprehended consciously, the archetypes, which inform them, are the elementary structures which are part of the unconscious and impossible to apprehend. Being part of the unconscious, the existence of archetypes can only be deduced indirectly by examining behaviour, images, art, myths, etc.

Archetype has its sources in anthropology and in Jungian theory. An archetype is the first real example or prototype of something. In this sense an archetype can be considered the ideal model, the supreme type or the perfect image of something. The term has been defined as a 'primordial image' that transcends the individual experience. Jung first referred to these as 'primordial images', a term he borrowed from Jacob Burckhardt. Later in 1917, he called them 'dominants' of the collective unconscious. It was not until 1919 that he first used the term 'archetypes' in an essay titled *Instinct and the Unconscious.*

Archetypes determine the form of imagery, rather than content. They are inferred from the vast range of concrete images and symbols found in mythologies, religions, dreams and art across history and space. An archetype appears in myths, but can also be seen its thematic or figurative dimension in literature, involving exile, rebirth, earth, goddess, etc.

According to Carl Jung, archetypes are structures, forming elements within the unconscious and give life to the images of both individual fantasies as well as to the mythologies of an entire culture. He also explains that archetypes are not inherited ideas or patterns of thought, but rather they are predisposed to respond in similar ways to certain stimuli. In reality "they belong to the realm of activities of the instincts and in that sense they represent inherited forms of psychic behaviour" (in Wilfred Guerin, *et al*, 1999, 178). Jung also used the term to refer to a recurring universal image, pattern, or motif representing a typical human experience. It is this aspect that gives archetypes their power - the ability to evoke themes that a vast majority of people can relate to what Jung wrote:

> There are as many archetypes as there are typical situations in life. Endless repetition has engraved these experiences into our psychic constitution, not in the forms of images filled with content, but at first only as forms without content, representing merely the possibility of a certain type of perception and action (1968, 3-4).

Archetypes are, according to Carl Jung, innate universal psychic dispositions that form the basic themes of human life. Each stage is mediated through a new set of archetypal imperatives which seek fulfillment in action. These may include being parented, initiation, acts of courtship, rituals associated with marriage and preparation for death.

In *The Power of Myth,* Campbell defines archetypes as elementary ideas or ground ideas. He suggests that 'archetype' is a better term because 'elementary idea' suggests headwork. Archetype of the unconscious means it comes from below. The difference between the Jungian archetypes of the unconscious and Freud's complexes is that the archetypes of the unconscious are manifestations of the organs of the body and their powers. Archetypes are biologically grounded, whereas the Freudian unconscious is a collection of repressed traumatic experiences from an individual's lifetime. The Freudian unconscious is a personal unconscious, it is biographical. The Jungian archetypes of the unconscious are biological. The biographical is secondary to that (Campbell, *et al*, 1991, 60-61).

According to Esther Lombardi, an archetype is a symbol that appears in literature, but there are also generalized patterns of archetypes that can be found through time and across cultures. When we study literature, these symbolic threads can be seen in plot elements, the setting or background, and/or in character development. The development of these characters in a work of literature may be done on an unconscious level by the author; the author may recognize a pattern in work and further build upon it to accomplish a desired dramatic effect.

For Northrop Frye the word 'archetype' means the first, the major or the ruling example or the pattern. The original patterns of myths are changed through 'displacement', a term coined by the psycho analysts. It means that basic instinctual drives and goals are disguised or changed so that whatever is being wanted or said becomes more believable and more morally and aesthetically acceptable.

Frye points out that an archetype should be not only a unifying category of criticism, but itself a part of a total form and it leads us at once to the question of what sort of total form criticism can see in literature. Total literary history moves from the primitive to the sophisticated, and here we glimpse the possibility of seeing literature as a complication of a relatively restricted and simple group of formulas that can be studied in primitive culture. If so, then the search for archetypes is a kind of literary anthropology, concerned with the way that literature is informed by pre-literary categories such as ritual, myth and folk tale (Northrop Frye, 1951, 99).

In *Northrop Frye on Culture and Literature* (1978), Robert Denham points out that Archetypes are easily locatable in highly conventionalized literatures which mean, for the most part, naïve, primitive, or popular literatures. Frye on the other hand distinguishes two kinds of archetypes: 'structural' or 'narrative archetypes' with a ritual content, and 'modal' or 'emblematic archetypes' in the drama of the educated audience and the settled theatre, in naïve or spectacular drama folk plays, puppet shows, pantomimes, farces, pageants, and their descendants in masques, comic operas, and commercial movies. Modal archetypes are best studied in naïve romance, which includes the folktales and fairytales that are so closely related to dreams of wonderful wishes coming true and to nightmares of ogres and witches (1978, 124-25).

The anthropological origins of archetypal criticism can pre-date its psychoanalytic origins by over thirty years. *The Golden Bough*, written by the Scottish anthropologist James G. Frazer, was the first influential text dealing with cultural mythologies. *The Golden Bough* was widely accepted as the seminal text on myth that spawned numerous studies on the same subject.

While Frazer's work deals with mythology and archetypes in material terms, the work of Carl Gustav Jung is, in contrast, immaterial in its focus. Jung's work theorizes myths and archetypes in relation to the unconscious, an inaccessible part of the mind. From a Jungian perspective, myths are the culturally elaborated representations of the contents of the deepest recess of the human psyche: the world of the archetypes.

The archetype to which Jung refers is represented through primordial images, a term he coined. Primordial images originate from the initial stages of humanity and have been part of the collective unconscious ever since. It is through primordial images that universal archetypes are experienced, and more importantly, that the unconscious is revealed.

Like the death-rebirth myth that Frazer sees as being representative of the growing seasons and agriculture as a point of comparison, Jungian analysis[5] envisions the death-

---

[5] Jungian psychoanalysis distinguishes between the personal and collective unconscious, the latter being particularly relevant to archetypal criticism. The collective unconscious, or the objective psyche as it is less frequently known, is a number of innate thoughts, feelings, instincts, and memories that reside in the unconsciousness of all people. Jung's definition of the term is inconsistent in his many writings. At one time he calls the collective unconscious the "a priori"- inborn forms of intuition, while in another instance it is a series of experiences that come upon us like fate. It is quite impossible to conceive how "experience" could originate exclusively in the outside world.

rebirth archetype as a symbolic expression of a process taking place not in the world but in the mind (Jung, 1968, 116).

2.4.1. Types of Archetypes

Jung described several archetypes based on the repeating patterns of thought and action that reappear time and again across people, countries and continents.

2.4.1.1. The shadow

The 'Shadow' is a very common archetype that reflects deeper elements of our psyche, where 'latent dispositions', which are common to us, all, arise. Our 'shadow' may appear in dreams, hallucinations and musings. It personifies everything that the subject refuses to acknowledge about himself and yet is always thrusting itself upon him directly or indirectly for instance inferior traits of character and other incompatible tendencies (Jung, 1968, 284-85).

2.4.1.2. The Anima/Animus

For Jung the second most prevalent pattern is that of the Anima (male), Animus (female), or, more simply, the Soul. It is the route to communication with the collective unconscious. The anima/animus represents our true self

---

The psyche is part of the inmost mystery of life, and it has its own peculiar structure and form like every other organism (Jung, 1968, 101).

considered to be as opposed to the masks we wear every day and is the source of our creativity. Turned towards the world, the anima is fickle, capricious, moody, uncontrolled and emotional, sometimes gifted with daemonic intuitions, ruthless, malicious, and obstinate, harping on principles, laying down the law, dogmatic, world-reforming, theoretic, word-mongering, argumentative, and domineering (1968, 124).

Anima and animus are male and female principles that represent a deep difference. Whilst men have a fundamental anima and women an animus, each may also have the other, just as men have a feminine side and women a masculine. Jung saw men as having one dominant anima, contributed by female members of his family, whilst women have a more complex, variable animus, perhaps made of several parts.

In combination, the anima and animus are known as syzygy (Jung, 1968, 67) a word also used to denote alignment of planets, representing wholeness and completion. This combining brings great power and can be found in religious combinations such as the Christian Holy Trinity (Father, Son and the Holy Ghost). A perfect partnership between man and woman can take place when not only our physical forms are compatible but also the *anima* and *animus.*

For Jung, the self is not just 'me' but God. It is the spirit that connects and is part of the universe. It is the coherent whole that unifies both consciousness and unconsciousness. It may be found elsewhere in such principles as nirvana and ecstatic harmony. It is perhaps what Jacques Lucan called 'the real'.

2.4.1.3. Family Archetype

Jung said that there are a large number of archetypes. These are often linked to the main archetypes and may represent aspects of them. They also overlap and many can appear in the same person. For example: A family archetype consists of the father, mother and the child. The father represents the dynamism of the archetype (Jung, 1968, 102); he also represents sternness and power. The qualities associated with the mother archetype are maternal solicitude and sympathy; the magic authority of the female; the wisdom and spiritual exaltation that transcend reason; any helpful instinct or impulse; all that is benign, all that cherishes and sustains, that fosters growth and fertility (1968, 82). The archetype of 'child god' is extremely widespread and intimately bound up with all the other mythological aspects of the child motif (1968, 158). The 'child' symbolizes the post conscious essence which is the essence of man. His preconscious essence is the unconscious state of earliest childhood; his post conscious essence is the anticipation by analogy of life after death (1968, 178).

2.4.1.4. Trickster

Archetypes consists stories of the wise old man who appears when the hero is in distress. He is the superior master and teacher, the father of the soul, and yet the soul, in some miraculous manner, is also his virgin mother, for which reason he is called by the alchemist the 'first son of the mother' (1968, 35). The Earth mother is always chthonic and is occasionally related to the moon, either through the blood sacrifice or through a child sacrifice, or else she is adorned with a sickle moon (1968, 185). The Earth Mother plays an important part in the woman's unconscious, for all her manifestations are described as 'powerful' (1968, 186). The hero is the rescuer and the champion. The hunter or old magician and the witch correspond to the negative parental images in the magic world of the unconscious (1968, 235). The trickster is someone who is 'fooled' or 'cheated'. He is known for his sly jokes and malicious pranks, his powers as a shape-shifter, his dual nature, half animal and half divine (1968, 255).

2.4.1.5. Animal Archetype

In Animal archetypes we encounter animals that act like humans, speak a human language, and display sagacity and knowledge superior to men (Jung 1968, 231). The archetype of the spirit is being expressed through an animal form. The three-legged and four-legged horses are in truth a recondite matter worthy of closer examination. Three-leggedness, as the attribute of some animal, denotes the unconscious masculinity immanent in a female creature[6] (Jung, 1968, 244).

In earlier work, Jung linked the archetypes to heredity and considered them as instinctual. Yet wherever he looked across cultures, he found the same archetypes and thus came to conceptualize them as fundamental forces that somehow exist beyond us. They have existed in ancient

---

[6]   A notable characteristic of Jung's archetypes is that we recognize them in image and emotion. This gives a profound effect on us and implies that they have deep and primitive origins. They thus have a particular potential for significance and may be feared or revered as mysterious signifiers of things beyond our complete understanding.

myths as elemental spirits and Jung sought to link with this deep and old experience.

It was not until the work of the Canadian literary critic Northrop Frye that archetypal criticism was theorized in purely literary terms. The major work of Frye's which deal with archetypes is not only the *Anatomy of Criticism* but his essay *The Archetypes of Literature* is a precursor to the book. Frye's thesis in *The Archetypes of Literature* remains largely unchanged in *Anatomy of Criticism*. Frye's work helped displace New Criticism as the major mode of analyzing literary texts, before giving way to structuralism and semiotics.

Frye's work breaks from both Frazer and Jung in such a way that it is distinct from its anthropological and psychoanalytical precursors. As for Jung, Frye was uninterested about the collective unconscious on the grounds of feeling it was unnecessary: since the unconscious is unknowable it cannot be studied. How archetypes came to be was also of no concern to Frye; rather, the function and effect of archetypes is his interest. For Frye, literary archetypes play an essential role in refashioning the material universe into an alternative verbal universe that is humanly intelligible and viable, because it is adapted to essential human needs and concerns.

2.4.1.6. Comedic and Tragic Categories

There are two basic categories in Frye's framework, comedic and tragic. Each category is further subdivided into two categories that are comedy and romance for the comedic; tragedy and satire for the tragic. Though he is dismissive of Frazer, Frye uses the seasons in his archetypal schema. Each season is aligned with a literary genre:

romance with spring, comedy with summer, tragedy with autumn, and satire with winter (Frye, 1951, 104).

Romance is aligned with spring because the genre of romance is characterized by the birth of the hero, revival and resurrection. Also, spring symbolizes the defeat of winter and darkness. Comedy and summer are paired together because summer is the culmination of life in the seasonal calendar, and the romance genre culminates with some sort of triumph, usually a marriage. Autumn is the dying stage of the seasonal calendar, which parallels the tragedy genre because it is, above all, known for the 'fall' or demise of the protagonist. Satire is metonomized with winter on the grounds that satire is a 'dark' genre; satire is a disillusioned and mocking form of the three other genres. It is noted for its darkness, dissolution, the return of chaos, and the defeat of the heroic figure.

Frye outlines five different spheres in his schema: human, animal, vegetation, mineral, and water. The comedic human world is representative of wish fulfillment and being community centred. In the tragic, human world is a tyranny or anarchy, or an individual or isolated man, the bullying giant of romance, the deserted or the betrayed hero. The animal world is a community of domesticated animals, usually a flock of sheep, or a lamb, or one of the gentler birds, usually a dove. The tragic, animal world is seen in terms of beasts and birds of prey, wolves, vultures, serpents, dragons and the like. The vegetable world is a garden, grove or park, or a tree of life, or a rose or lotus. In the tragic, it is sinister forest or heath or wilderness, or a tree of death. Cities with the 'starlit dome' or building or temple, or one stone, normally a glowing precious stone represent the comedic images. In the tragic vision the mineral world is seen in terms of deserts, rocks and ruins, or of sinister geometrical images like the cross. Lastly the unformed world is a river, traditionally fourfold. This world usually becomes the sea, as the narrative myth of dissolution is so often a flood myth. The combination of the sea and beast images gives us the leviathan and similar water monster (Frye, 1951, 108-110).

Archetypal literary criticism is a type of critical theory that interprets a text by focusing on recurring myths and archetypes in the narrative, symbols, images, and character types in a literary work. Archetypal literary criticism's origins are rooted in two other academic disciplines, social anthropology and psychoanalysis. Archetypal criticism was its most popular in the 1950's and 1960's, largely due to Northrop Frye.

2.5. Unus Mundus

Jung proposed that the archetype had a dual nature: it exists both in the psyche and in the world at large. He called this non-psychic aspect of the archetype the *psychoid* archetype. Jung used the ancient term of *unus mundus*; to describe the unitary reality which he believed underlay all manifest phenomena. He conceived archetypes to be the mediators of the *unus mundus*, organizing not only ideas in the psyche, but also the fundamental principles of matter and energy in the physical world. For the *A·chiks*, tradition, myth and religion are inseparably intermingled. The *A·chiks* believe that the soul of a person is not being perished at death but the soul remains and turns into a process of forming a new flesh and body through reincarnation. For them the spirit and life after death is real, hence the rituals to bring back home, the surviving members take upon themselves the responsibility of looking after the spirit and sending it off to live among other spirits. If this ritual is not performed, the spirit wanders about on earth and takes long time to reach its destination.

Archetypal pedagogy was developed by Clifford Mayes, which bears some similarities to the pedagogical approach proposed by the French Jungian psychologist Frederic Fappani. Frederic Fappani, as a neo-Jungian scholar, has produced the first book-length studies in French on the pedagogical implications and applications of Jungian and neo-Jungian psychology, which is based on the work of Carl Gustav Jung (1875-1961). Jungian psychology is also called analytical psychology. He has developed what he has termed Jungienne education that envision a pedagogy which helps students explore those ultimate concerns in a way that is spiritually sensitive without being theologically dogmatic or denominationally partisan (Mayes, 2005, 40).

All the most powerful ideas in history go back to archetypes. This is particularly true of religious ideas, but the central concepts of science, philosophy, and ethics are no exception to this rule. In their present form they are variants of archetypal ideas created by consciously applying and adapting these ideas to reality. For it is the function of consciousness not only to recognize and assimilate the external world through the gateway of the senses, but also to translate into visible reality the world within us.

Archetypal criticism argues that archetypes determine the form and function of literary works that a text's meaning is shaped by cultural and psychological myths. Archetypes are the unknowable basic forms personified or concretized in recurring images, symbols, or patterns which may include motifs such as the quest or the heavenly ascent, recognizable character types such as the trickster or the hero, symbols such as the apple or snake, or images such as crucifixion all laden with meaning already when employed in a particular work.

Archetypal critics find New Criticism to be too atomistic in ignoring inters to be textual elements and in approaching the text as if it existed in a vacuum. After all, we recognize story patterns and symbolic associations at least from other texts we have read; we know how to form assumptions and expectations from encounters with black hats, springtime settings, evil stepmothers, and so forth. Archetypal images and story patterns encourage readers and viewers of films and advertisements to participate ritualistically in basic beliefs, fears, and anxieties of their age. These archetypal features not only constitute the intelligibility of the text but also tap into a level of desires and anxieties of humankind. The *A·chiks* have woven myths and archetypes around mystic and mysterious physical phenomena like that of the rivers, clouds, the thunder, lightning, the sun and stars, the hills and other natural formations to give plausible and imaginative explanations of their origin and existence, adding more mystery to them in the process.

Chapter III

Mapping the Garo (*A·chik*)
Traditions in Folk Narratives

Garo Hills is situated between 25° 9' and 26° 1 of North latitude and between 89° 49' and 91° 2' of East Longitude. It is surrounded on the north and west by the district of Goalpara, Assam, on the south by the district of Mymensingh of Bangladesh and on the east by Khasi Hills of Meghalaya State. The entire district is densely wooded and bordered by patches of hollow and swamps but due to the *Jhum* or shifting cultivation, virgin forests and ancient trees have disappeared except in the reserves. Agriculture is the mainstay of *A·chik* economy.

The *A·chik* society is a matrilineal society and its descent is traced through the mother and the residence is also matrilocal. The title is also taken from mother's side which is known as *Ma·chong*. The inheritance to the family property goes to the female line through the daughter. The *A·chik* society divides themselves mainly into two clans (*chatchi*) - such as Marak and Sangma but nowadays, we find other clans such as Momin, Shira, Arengh added to the *A·chik* clan (Julius Marak, 2000, 4).

A major ethnic community of the North East, the *A·chiks* has no written history but then they have a vibrating legacy of cultural and social life-world. Their life world is intimately associated with myriad narratives, folklores and mythical universe and age old social customs. Their rich cultural heritage is explored by folk narratives. Access to their recess of their folk world is the only way to comprehend the mystic as well as the mythical folk world of the community. Hence, an engagement with the ethnic life world of the *A·chiks* makes understanding of the folklore studies as a tool into an academic imperative.

Major A. Playfair in *The Garos* (1998) says that as per the Garo tradition and legends, originally the *A·chiks* came from Tibet and settled down in Koch Behar, from where they moved on to Jogighopa. To escape from their oppressors they crossed the Brahmaputra on raft of plantain stems. They are then believed to have marched towards Guwahati. They next wandered and settled in the neighbourhood of Boko in the present district of Kamrup, Assam. The *A·chiks* are said to have established a kingdom in the Habraghat pargana of which the first reigning king was Habra or Abra. However, there arose some differences amongst the *A·chiks* in the Habraghat pargana, and it was because of this reason that some of them set out on their travels again and entered the Hills, presently known as Garo Hills (1998, 9-10).

Milton Sangma in his *History of Garo Literature* (1992) points out that *A·chik* is the language of the majority community of the Garo Hills district of Meghalaya. Grierson in his *Linguistic Survey of India* classified the *A·chik* language as a section the Bodo group of languages, which, in turn, is a branch of the Tibeto-Burman group of languages of the Tibeto-Chinese speech Family (6-8). In one of the earliest publications, *The Garo Jungle Book*, William Carey says that there are thirteen different dialects among the *A·chiks* (1993, 251). The *Am·bengs*[7]; the *A·kawes* or *A·wes*[8]; the *Chisaks*[9]; the *Duals* or *Matchi Dual*[10]; the *Matchis*[11]; the *Matjangchis* or *Matabengs*[12]; the *Chiboks*[13]; the

---

[7]   The *Am·bengs* are one of the sub-divisions of the *A·chik* tribe, who occupy the western portion of the Garo Hills district.

[8]   *A·kawe* means 'valley' or 'plain' and hence the *A·chik* dwellers of the valley or the plains. *A·we* means to 'plough by harrow' and so people who cultivate by plough are called the *A·wes*. They occupy the whole of the northern hills and the plains at their foot, from Kamrup district in the east to some distance west of the *Jinari* river.

[9]   The *Chisaks* occupy the north-eastern hills, from the southern border of the *a·wes* in the north, to within a few miles of the *Simsang* river in the south; and from the western border of the Khasi hills in the east to about thrity miles westwards. *Chi* means 'water' and *sak* means 'above'. Therefore, *Chisak* refers to the *A·chiks* inhabiting the areas above the water sources.

[10]   The *Dual* villages are situated on the banks of the *Simsang* river and in the hills close to the south bank of the river where it turns towards the plains. A large number of this subtribe dwells in the plains in the Mymensingh district of Bangladesh.

[11]   The central valley of the Simsang to the west of the *Duals* is inhabited by the *Matchis*. They spread towards the north touching the *a·wes*, and southward, up to the northern slopes of the central range of high hills. They occupy the heart of Garo Hills.

[12]   The *Matjangchis* or *Matabengs* are found in the north of *Simsang* river. They live between the *Matchis* and *A·bengs*. Major playfair is of the opinion that though they claim to be of a distinct division, their language and geographical distribution make it more than likely that there is a mingling of the *A·bengs* and the *Matchis* in them.

[13]   The *Chiboks* live immediately to the east of the *A·bengs*, in the

Rugas[14]*;* the *Garas* or *Ganchings*[15]*;* the *Atongs*[16]. To these may be added another which is called *Me·gam*[17] that is found along the Garo-Khasi Hills border (Playair, 1998, 59-60).

---

upper valley of the *Bogai* river and extends eastward to the Nitai river. The *Chiboks* are few in number and their myths and general culture show considerable variations from those of other *A·chiks*. Their folk dances are distinct from the dances of the other *A·chiks*.

[14] The *Rugas* reside to the south of the *Chiboks*, in the low hills bordering on the Mymensingh district, in the vicinity of Dalu. They differ considerably from the other *A·chiks* in their general culture.

[15] The areas to the south of the main range, extending from *Nitai Nitai* river nearly to the *Simsang* river is inhabited by the *Ganchings*, or as they are called the *Garas*.

[16] They form an important division of the tribe and occupy the *Simsang* valley and the hills in the vicinity as far as north Siju. They are different from other division of the tribe especially in their dialect. Major Playfair is of the opinion that their dialect is nearer to the *Koch* language that to the other *A·chik* dialects. The other *A·chiks* hardly understand their language.

[17] They are found on the eastern border of the Garo Hills district, from Kamrup in the north to Mymensingh in the south. They also inhabit the valley of the *Rongkai* stream and valleys around the foot of *Balpakram* hills. The *Megams* are called *Lyngams* by the *Khasis*. They seem to be a fusion of the *A·chiks* and *Khasi* and can be taken as hybrid race. In appearance and customs, they closely resemble the *A·chiks*, but their language has been classified by Dr. Grierson as *Khasi*. They have their own dialect which cannot be understood by the *A·chiks*. Their social structure is similar to that of the *A·chiks*. They have the same exogamous division namely, Sangma and Marak, as the *A·chiks*.

The *A·chiks* do not have a rich literary tradition in the written form; neither do they have a script of their own. According to Dewansing Rongmuthu, there exists, however, a belief among some sections of the *A·chiks* that they possessed a literature of their own in their own script and language on rolls of parchment made from the skins of animals. The literature was evolved while they were still in Mandalay, in Upper Burma. When they left Tibet and wandered towards the plains of India, they faced acute shortage of food, and so they boiled those scrolls of parchments and ate them up (2008,1-2). The *A·chiks* evolved Oral literature which was tenaciously handed down from one generation to another orally due to lack of script. The *A·chiks* possess a large number of verses and stories, folktales, myths, songs, prayers etc. that formed the oral literature of the tribe.

The traditional or old *A·chik* literature consists of historical accounts, legends, myths and tales told in poetry as well as in prose, various kinds of songs sung on different occasions as well as in the sacrificial ceremonies. Since the written script was yet to be developed, the traditional materials remained eventually oral, hence, the traditional literature survives to this day in the interior places where the traditional faith of the *A·chiks* is still held and old customs and practices persist. This poetry or song can be defined as the *Volkseele* of the *A·chik* through which they narrate the approximation of their soul with their mystic reality. Various forms of songs and prayers may be said to have constituted the traditional *A·chik* poetry like the prayers during sacrificial ceremonies connected with *jhum* cultivation, song of inaugurating a house, *Dani Doka* of the *Wangala* or harvest festival, *Ajea* is an essential feature of the *Wangala* and the funeral wails *Grapmangtata* or *Kabe*.

The sacrificial songs are solemn prayers to powerful unseen divinities in the *A·chik* pantheon. They collectively form the grand unwritten mantra-shastra, the sacred hymns or odes of the *A·chiks*. Only a *Kamal* or priest can ordinarily chant out or sing the sacrificial songs, although they are handed down from generation to generation by word of mouth. It would indeed be a sacrilege to call them folk songs. Songs are considered as the vehicles through which human beings communicated with one another as well as with nature which was seen as the personification of God.

Traditionally, the sacrificial songs are the sacred words of argument, only which the deities can understand. It is believed by the *A·chiks* that misuse of their holy sacrificial songs, which is a taboo for laymen to sing or chant out ordinarily, brings down appropriate punishments in forms of fatal illness, maiming or blindness. Almost all notable sacrificial ceremonies of the *A·chiks* involve ritual dances. But, on any occasion, the sacred sacrificial songs of the *A·chiks* are never commonly sung or chanted out by the laity (Rongmuthu, 1996, 12). Iris Watre in *Music and Musical Instruments of the Garo Tribe of North-East* (2007) mentions how the songs were also used for renewing the fertility of soil and crops, for invoking the spirit - gods for exhibiting magical feats and even for curing the diseases (26). There are also songs which are independent of specific occasions and are sung at any convenient time and place, they are: *Katta Salling* - The narrative of *Salling*, *Katta Agana* or The Epic Story Narration, Folk Songs - *Nanggorere*, *Gonda Doka*, *Gogaia Gosaia*.

Traditional poetry, thus, is a true mirror of the typical *A·chik* way of life, their social and religious practices. It is a record of what the *A·chik* ancestors thought and believed, and a key to the understanding of *A·chik* psyche. The various forms of traditional poetry reflect how the sensibility of the *A·chik* people responded to the world or nature and to their environment. In the *A·chik* tradition poetry is a medium through which they express their joys and sorrows.

In *Influence of English on Garo Poetry* (1985) Caroline Marak says that prayers during a sacrificial ceremony connected with *jhum* cultivation are performed at every stage of *jhum* cultivation. These ceremonies begin from cutting a few bushes to indicate that a particular area is reserved for clearing by a certain family, to the time of depositing the harvest in the granary. These ceremonies, in successive order are *O·pata, Den·bilsia, A·siroka, A·galmaka, Mi Amua, Rongchu Gala* or *Ginde Gala, Ahaia, Wangala* and *Rusrota*. Some of these ceremonies are performed by the priest, some by the *Nokma* or the village headman, and others by the head of the family (1985, 38).

3.1. *Krita – Amua*

Krita or *Amua* are ceremonies connected with *Jhum* Cultivation. The first of invocational songs we come across during the agricultural cycle is the *A·a o·pata*. According to the story of creation it is believed that it was the deity *Tatara Rabuga Stura Pantura* who created the earth or ground and water. Then it was the deity *Jipjini Jipjana* who created the lives on the earth above and in the waters below. It was the *Asima Dingsima Dramma Chisama Den·pema Den·jima*, the spirit or deity, who created the trees and the shrubs. After all these creation only the spirit *Abetpa Ranggapa* was assigned by *Tatara Rabuga Stura Pantura* to look after the land, forests, springs, hills and valleys, etc. Therefore, if any person without any consultation with this spirit clears the plot of land, the assigned spirit will be wrathful and he may even cause illness or death (Paulinus Marak, 2005, 49-50). After having chosen the plot, clearing of the jungle takes place. That patch of land may be the habitation of a malignant deity, known as *Abet Rora Raka Ganda*. So, on cutting the first plants for clearing, he utters the following address to the *Abet Rora* and *Raka Ganda*:

> Thou *Abet Rora*, Thou *Raka Ganda*…
> Yet, thou *Abet Rengge*
> This place I will clear up…
> I will (herein) dig up and cover,
> And conceal (cereal seeds)
> Hast thou heard me?
> > (Rongmuthu, 1996, 14).

Then the householder goes home and waits for a dream for a night or two. If he has unlucky dream, he abandons the spot and searches for another. But, if the dream is a good one, he sets to work on it. The ceremony starts after clearing the jungles for *jhum* cultivation. This is known as *Den·bilsia* or *A·a bakchata*, which also signifies the driving off of all uncleanness and disease and to invoke the god of human lives to free them from all misfortunes. Hence the performer makes the symbolic act of spitting out water saying *Poi* (utterance which accompanies the spitting out of water) from a new bamboo tube container made especially for the occasion. The chant is of course, accompanied by libation. They not only clear their *jhum* fields at this time, but also their homes and surrounding areas. This is followed by the *jhum* burning ceremony called *A·siroka*, during which the following incantation is used to call the goddess of *Minimaa Kiri Rokkime*. *A·siroka* a sacrificial chant to *Rokkime* the goddess of rice, to come and make her abode in the field: "Make rice to grow bountifully, cause cotton to blossom and bear fruits abundantly" (qtd. in Caroline Marak, 1985, 39). Before she can come and dwell the land must be cleansed of profanation due to evil acts like bloodshed or suicide that may have been committed there. The prayer has two parts, the first part is intended to drive away the desecration and the second is a supplication to the goddess for abundance of crops (40).

Just before the ceremony the father of the house calls out all the inmates of the house and asks them to go to the field. When all the members of the house arrive at the *jhum* field, he calls upon the mother of the god of fire, *Sre-Tonggitchak-Gitok-Warikat* to free the *jhum* land from any profanation, pollution and desecration (Wa·tre, 2007, 15). Each householder performs first the ceremony on his newly made field and is performed at household level in the morning. At noon the ceremony is repeated in each household. For the purpose of performance of the *A·galmak Krita* a householder erects a fresh altar of culms of bamboo and *araru* or *bengraru* (an order of palm) on a selected site in the field. He chants out sacrificial songs over burning incense at the altar of *Minimaa Rokkime*, the Mother of rice. He kills domestic animals as sacrificial offerings and smears their blood at the altar. At the permanent altar by the *turumal* (the main central pillar of the house), the householder chants out sacrificial songs to *Minimaa Rokkime*. To the *A·chiks*, *Minimaa Rokkime*, the mother of rice and Goddess of wealth, is the ideal personification of all that is beauteous, auspicious, desired and desirable in worldly terms. The villagers at first congregate in the house of the village *A·king (land) Nokma* for the ceremonial performance. With the ritual burnings at the home altar and chanting sacrificial songs, the *kram achok* or *kram bichok* (Sacred drum), the *rangs* (basin-like lead-brass gongs) and the *adils* (trumpet made of buffalo horn) are sounded (Rongmuthu, 1996, 16- 17).

The time when the seeds sprout and grow into young shoots is considered the most vulnerable period for the plants by the *A·chiks*. Thus they have a special ceremony and it is known as *Me·jak sim·a*. The aim of the sacrifice is an offering to the deity of crops so that she may protect the crops from every possible destruction caused by insects, moths, animals, failure of rain, etc. The *A·chiks* believe that whatever works are done without the blessing and divine assistance are not fruitful. In order to get fruitful harvest and protection of the crops by the divine assistance this particular sacrifice is performed (Paulinus Marak, 2005, 54). The following incantation is used to call up the goddess *Minimaa Rokkime* to dwell in their land and to bless them with good harvest:

> Oh! *Rokkime*, the god of food grains of rice, come and bless our crops of the field and comfort us in our sorrows. The rice barns are beside the streamlets waiting for you to bless them (qtd. in Julius Marak, 2000, 66).

The *A·chiks* generally follow multi-crop system, wherein the various seeds are sown. The *kamal* (priest) takes a lump of earth from the field and naming the various curses goes around the land. He puts the lump of earth in a *koksep* (a bamboo basket with a lid) and shouts saying all the curses and disease have been put in. Then the prayer is chanted:

> Do not shrivel and wither away
> Within my field and its boundaries.
> Let the paddy grow lush and green

Like the green back of the parrot.
Shoo! Be gone you demon.
    (qtd. in Wa·tre, 2007, 29)

The *A·chiks* believe that *Akkal* or *Bang* or *Rakasi* is the fiend of famine. It is a malignant spirit, which sucks away the vital principle or rice. It thus brings about famine or acute food scarcity to humankind. The sacrificial ceremony of the *Akkal gala* is performed partly in the *jhum* fields and partly at home. Fresh altars of bamboo culms and *bengraru* or *araru* are erected in the *jhum* field and in the house of each cultivator of the village. To begin festivities and ritual dances the villagers congregate the house of the village *A·king Nokma* at noon. With chanting of sacrificial songs over burning incense at the home altar, rhythmic sounds of traditional musical instruments begin.

Having assured the safe growth of the plants, we come to the harvest time. The first fruits are never eaten but are first given as thanks offering to *Misi Saljong*, the sun god, who first taught humankind the art of cultivation and also provided seed grains to humankind. This ceremony is called *Rongchu gala* (offering of the flattened rice). The *Rongchu gala* is also called *Ginde gala* (offering of rice flour). The ceremony is always initiated by the *Nokma* (village headman). The chant recited at this time say:

Bestower of blessings, sower and planter,
Katchi Beari (demon) and *Susime* (the Moon God)
Partake of this food and rice-beer
Which we will not eat or drink before you.
But shall have with you.
    (qtd. in Wa·tre, 2007, 30)

With ritual incense burning, chanting of sacrificial songs and ritual token offerings of flattened rice, rice-flour and rice-beer at the home-altar, the rhythmic sounds of traditional musical instruments begin and rice-beer prepared out of the first fruits is drawn and served out to all assembled guests. The householder grasps *mi·lam* (double-edged *A·chik* sword) and *spi* (rectangular *A·chik* shield) in his hands, and amidst rhythmic sounds of traditional musical instruments, performs ritual dance before the admiring audience.

A special ceremony is performed during the reaping of the *jhum* paddy. This is called *Ja·megapa* or *Megap ra·ona* and is also called *Ahaia*. Best selected sheaves of paddy, out of the year's *jhum* field are used to be kept hanging by the roof inside the temporary shelter in the *jhum* fields till the paddy harvest is completed. The paddy sheaves are ceremoniously brought down from their pensile resting places to the accompaniment of sacrificial songs, on the day of completion of paddy harvest in the *jhum* cultivations. It is interesting to note that, while the sheaves of paddy are being brought in, the children follow the person carrying the sheaves, uttering the words *Ahoea, Ahoea*. The paddy sheaves are put down around the home-altar beside the *turumal* (the main central post of a dwelling house). More quantities of incense are added to the fire in the brazier and sacrificial songs, invoking *Minimaa Rokkime*, the Mother of rice, to dwell in the house and in the family granary, and *Na·ma Na·sa* (the mother of fish), to abide in the waters of the homeland are chanted out over burning incense. This is probably the sequel to the sing song that takes place in the evening, between the young men and maidens of the village. The song that is usually sung is known as *Ahoea* (Wa·tre, 2007, 31). In this way the *A·chiks* maintain their peaceful relationship with the supernatural beings which surround them. If they do not maintain such relationship they believe that the deities or the spirits may be offended and as a result any kind of suffering may be brought to the transgressor.

Finally, we come to the biggest of the festivals of the *A.chiks* - the *Wangala* or harvest festival. This is also known by other names such as *Drua Wanbola* and *Wanna Rongchua*. This is a 'thanksgiving' as well as 'Send-off-ceremony' to bid farewell to *Minimaa Rokkime* (mother of paddy) and *Misi Saljong* (god of food crops) who would return to their respective homelands somewhere in the universe, after the harvest is over. The days of *Wangala* are holy unto *Misi Saljong Jobepa Rangrupa* and to *Minimaa Rokkime*, the benign divinities of the *A·chiks*. The days are meant to eat, drink, dance, and sing and to make great mirth. The *A·chiks* believe that the *Wangala* is a joy to *Misi Saljong* and the joy of *Misi Saljong* is the strength of the *A·chiks*. They also believe that *Misi Saljong* pours out untold blessings to the dutiful and the industrious *jhum* cultivators. The spirit of the *Wangala* is, therefore, a perfect negation of despair and despondency, of hatred and bitterness. The *A·chiks* refuse to believe that, under the abiding benign influence of *Misi Saljong*, the most powerful Divinity of Light and Fertility, for whom the *Wangala* is dedicated, the forces of darkness will ever overwhelm the *A·chik* race. The *Wangala* forcefully drives home that evil cannot completely eclipse the good and that the strong, the courageous, the fortitudinous, the upright and the chaste know no defeat. At this time, an important ceremony is performed known as *Kumanchi Wal·dukaa*, which literally means negotiation between God and humankind, where a special request is made to the gods to return in the next season (Wa·tre, 2007, 31).

3.2. Song on Inauguration of a House

Speaking about the song of inaugurating the house, Caroline Marak observes that at the completion of a house, the inauguration takes place usually in the evening. The ceremony of offering a chicken and libation inside the house is followed by the singing of the inaugural song. The master of the house or one familiar with the song leads the singing uttering the words: "As the father of *Mune* made the place his home" (1985, 41). The guests, squatting, sing responsibly, *a-a-a* at the end of each line and rap the bamboo floor with pieces of log to the rhythm of the song. When the ceremony is over, food is served and is followed by group dancing and the warrior dance. The singer states his determination to settle down in the village and cultivate the land. 'Shield' and 'Shade' are instances of *aganmitapa* (to speak behind the surface) in which the newly built house is compared to the source of protection from outside menace and the forces of nature. The implication is that the master of the house will dwell in the place and cultivate the land as his forefathers did in Garo Hills. The chanting is done with solemnity.

> I have a shield,
> I have a shade,
> I will also cultivate the land,
> I will also dwell in the village.
> (qtd. in Caroline Marak, 2004, 72).

In the traditional way he offers sacrifices of birds, smearing their blood and sticking their feathers on the walls. In this connection, allusions to the stories of the *A·chik* ancestors are made. According to the legend, *Mune* and *Sane* were the daughters of an *A·chik* forefather who practiced *jhum* cultivation. *Niba Jonja*[18] is said to be the first man to have acquired the *muni* and *chambuni* (the sleep inducing plants) which are also believed to cast a spell. He is said to have foiled the designs of *Salgra*, the Sungod, to carry his wife away by planting the *muni* on the path to his house.

> Formerly, as my father with the *muni*
> (a herb which is believed to induce sleep) of *Niba*
> In former days as my grandfather with the c*hambuni*
> of Jonja,
> I will pull out and play,
> I will play with small round clods
> For the land and the site of my house…
>   (qtd. in Caroline Marak, 2004, 72)

The mood of the song is one of gaiety, to suit the happy occasion. This prayer is part of the sacrificial ceremony made to *Misi Saljong*, the God who blesses and allots shares (Caroline Marak, 1985, 42).

3.3. *Dani*

Dani is a traditional *A·chik* song sung to a tune by elderly men, to the exclusion of women and young men. The singing of the *Dani* is a feature of the *Wangala* festival of harvest and thanksgiving to the gods. The men wearing various ornaments, arms on each other's shoulders, in conviviality pour the drink into each other's mouth from

---

[18] A myth is told about *Niba, Jonja*, a Garo patriarch, which he fought with *Salgra*, the sun-god with the herb *muni chambuni* – a herb which is believed to induce sleep.

their own *pong* (shell of small variety of gourd used for ladling and serving rice beer) While singing *Dani* one takes the lead in singing, saying the words, while others sing responsively, saying *Ho anga dania* or *Hai anga* as a refrain. The version of the *Dani* consists of three main elements: (i) the myth concerning the origin of the *Wangala* dance, (ii) the story of *Ase* and *Malja*, and (iii) origin of the thanksgiving ceremony to the gods for the harvest. These tales and the story of the *jhum* cultivation are woven together to make a colourful web. Each strand of the narrative is taken up or abandoned as desired by the singer (Caroline Marak, 1985, 43-44).

The song *Dani Doka* begins with the myth recalling the ancient origin of the *Wangala* dance. It was in the underworld, in the Country beneath the waters, in the land of the Mother and the waters of *Bidawe* that its inhabitants first demonstrated the art of dancing. The underworld was decked with precious stones. All the living beings of the earth and of the water for the first time performed the *Wangala*, dancing to the rhythm of the drum and playing musical instruments (Caroline Marak, 1985, 44).

> It was in the underworld,
> The land beneath the waters,
> In the land of the mother
> And the waters of *Bidawe*,
> That *Wangala* was first demonstrated.
>   (qtd. in Wa·tre, 2007, 40)

Noro, the first man did not know how to dance. He simply made human figures out of sand on the river bank, and put a reed on its head in place of feathers. He fashioned drum out of the bamboo tube. Not knowing how to make musical instruments, he made music with his mouth (Caroline Marak, 1985, 44).

The story *Wangala* is linked to the tale of *Ase* and *Malja*. In the beginning of the world, there was no sun or moon, days or months. Seeds of life and grains were yet to come. Thus, the ancient men used red earth for red grains of rice, and black earth for black rice. They gave nought to eat and nought to drink:

> Taking red earth of red rice,
> And black earth for black rice,
> They fed nought into the mouth,
> And served nought to drink.
> (qtd. in Caroline Marak, 1985, 45)

When they gave yellow water as wine, the spout of *pong* (shell of small variety of gourd used for ladling and serving rice beer) became wet and slippery. When they fed mud as rice, their hands were filled to overflowing. It was *Denjong Ganjong* who first divided and served mud as rice to others. *Ase*, a male relative and *Malja*, the son of *Dian Gancheng*, deliberately absented themselves. They would not partake of the food and refused to join the festivities. This was an act of irreverence to *Misi Saljong*, the god of blessing and distribution due to which both of them were defiled. The profanation resulted in *Ase* being killed by a tigress and *Malja* being taken by a mermaid:

> A tigress killed *Ase*;
> A mermaid took *Malja*.
> (qtd. in Caroline Marak, 1985, 46)

It was *Giri* and his nephew *Ringcha* who went and informed the widow, the *Bine* woman and the destitute *Kangse Tira* of the tragedy. The women, weeping in great sorrow, wondered who would search for their missing spouses. It was *Sirampa* and *Manggolpa* who traced the dead bodies. Birds and insects performed the death ceremonial rites (Caroline Marak, 1985, 46).

About the middle of the song, the myth concerning the origin of the *Cha·chat Soa* or the 'burning of the incense' ceremony is introduced along with the story of the *jhum* cultivation.

The god of blessings *Misi Saljong* made his sojourn in the house of the destitute widow *Ae* and *Ae Dikante*. They, being very poor, and having nothing to offer as gift to their guest *Saljong Racha Misi Gitel*, burnt incense for him at the *truma* or the central post erected beside the hearth in a typical *A·chik* house. The god was very pleased with them and blessed them with grains. From this offering originated the practice of the burning of the incense ceremony which is performed at the beginning of the *Wangala*. The god then departed for Mother *Nokki* and grandmother *Dimki*, to the country of *Achi* and the waters of *Dimchre*. Further *Misi Saljong* conferred favour upon *Gisil* and his maternal uncle *Pandil*. He took *Gisil* as his son-in-law and *Pandil* as husband to his daughter. The singer, recalling the ancient past, says that stone implements were used for tilling the land, and that the ancient men fought with stone weapons.

A year has passed since the clearing of the jungle for cultivation, the seeds sown in the field have borne fruits, and the harvest is over. The time has come for thanksgiving to

Misi Saljong, and the occasion calls for celebration. Gratitude to the goddess of rain is also expressed. The grains and cotton seeds have been sown in anticipation of rain and the hopes of the people have been fulfilled.

Another feature of the harvest season described by the singer is the destruction of the crops by wild animals. After giving a beautiful pictorial description of wild goats which live in steep slopes and cliffs, and fight with their horns locked together, tails bent down, he says that they come to the field and eat away the crops. Wild boars also destroy a part of the produce. The origin of the *jhum* cultivation is also recalled:

> The 'jhum' where trees were cut by *Bone*,
> The field cleared by *Jane*,
> Was cultivated,
> Seeds were sown.
>   (qtd. in Caroline Marak, 1985, 49)

These above lines refer to the story of *Bone Nirepa Jane Nitepa*, the man who is said to have pioneered in *jhum* cultivation, whose first field was *Misi Kokdok Abri* (the Hill of Six Basketfuls of Millet) in the north-east of Garo Hills (Caroline Marak, 1985, 49).

The *Dani* is appropriately brought to a close with the concluding lines recalling the origin of the *Wangala* dance once more. This song thus is steeped in the traditional myths and tales which are more or less familiar to the participants.

3.4. *Ajea*

Ajea can be said to be a kind of song. According to Caroline Marak, *Ajea* is a song chanted by an individual or by two participants in response to one another. The singing of *Ajea* is an essential feature of the *Wangala* and custom sanctions the informal get-together of the youth, their romance through the song and the possible selection of marriage partners (Caroline Marak, 1985, 49-50). If the song is centred around on any other theme other than love, then it can be sung on any ordinary occasion and it is known as *Ajeme·apa*. But if the song is sung during *Wangala*, it is called *Wangalao Ajea*. *Wangalao Ajea* can be sung between the two young lovers. In the *A·beng* area it is known as *Ajebalsala*.

Ajebalsala is a kind of wooing and proposal to enter into love and marriage. The young man and woman exchange their views and thoughts through the songs, they express their feelings for one another. *Ajebalsala* being an oral rendition, they can improvise the song but they follow the traditional pattern, they do not always invent. In ancient days, the young people cannot choose their life partners on their own; they are always bound by rules and laws. However, during *Wangala* they have freedom to choose.

The tone of *Ajea* is light hearted and gay, because this song is a source of amusement during the festivities, an opportunity for the youth to get acquainted with each other, and a way of releasing their emotions. Through *Ajea* the young woman of a particular village, asks the young boy in a typical manner from whence, how and why he came. They enquire about each others' clan, for then only will they know whether marriage is possible between them. According to *A·chik* customary laws, man and woman of the same clan are not eligible to marry. Accordingly, if marriage is possible between them, romance will develop, which is life-blood and source of inspiration of this form of *Ajea*. The song goes thus:

> Are you a parrot wandering aimlessly? From which
> kind of tree are you?
> Are you a hero without destination? From which
> village are you?
> Are you a mynah flying in from the plains?
> Have you come for the *Wangala* of the *Nokma*?
>   (Caroline Marak, 1985, 51)

Thus the girl by means of beautiful imagery asks whence he come, whether he has come with the purpose of participating in the *Wangala* festival, dressed and prepared for the festival. In this way they sing and respond to each other and their romance develop through songs. The song becomes deeper and deeper that at last they make commitment to each other.

> By one path let us run away my dear
> And together die in one pyre, my dear.
>   (Caroline Marak, 1985, 55)

Proposals made by both the girl and the boy are part of the song. They express their love, admiration and desire for each other and their songs culminate in their intention to elope and marry. The following lines express how the boy is attracted and falls in love even with the glance of the young girl. Her conversation with him and others leads him to love.

I have fallen for (her) very glance

And her utterance has endeared her (to me)

    (Dhoronsingh, 1974, 52).

With the approval of the *Nokma* and relatives, the romantic desires of a couple finds fulfillment and ends in marriage. Through the song, the *A·chiks* can find their life partners. The song is a source of amusement during the festivals.

3.5. Dirge or *Kabe* or *Grapmangtata*

Dirge or *Grapmangtatta* or *Kabe* or *Grapmikchi* is steeped in traditional *A·chik* beliefs regarding life after death, spirits, reincarnation and the cause of death. *Grapmangtata* literally means lament - it is a funeral dirge. It is a song of lamentation at the death of a loved one. The out pouring of a broken heart is encapsulated in *Kabe*.

3.5.1. Myth of *Kabe*

Mihir N Sangma in his book *Pagitchamni Ku·bisring* (1996, 47) speaks about the origin of *Kabe*. He says that a man *Demi Resi* (the ancient man) called *Eman Me·a Banggi Me·chik* lived in the deep pool called *Dengreng Wari* in the *Rompa* stream which joins the *Simsang* river. The story says that one day *Eman Me·a* heard *kabe* for the first time which was coming from the distant forest. Mistaking the voice that was crying with painful heart to be a human voice, he kept silent in fear. But it was a bird named *Gangsime Gangchime* (*renggok bima*/the female hornbill) (Mihir Sangma, 1996, 45) which fully moved him and made him forget his way back home and also where he was heading to. After hearing the voice of the bird, he further looked around and found the bird just a short distance from the stream. The bird had died with his wings spread open toppled over by a stone. The female bird had gone through such painful days of hunger and thirst that she could no longer bear it. At the same time, *Bangji Me·chik*, the wife of *Dema Resi Eman Me·a*, thought that her husband has lost his way in the deep forest. Out of fear and despair, she informed the villagers. As soon as they heard the news, though it was dangerous to search for him in the deep forest at night, they went out with their *bilcham* (traditional torches) to look for him. Though late, he reached home safely. He related the real story to his wife as he lay down to sleep after dinner. After the story of the bird was narrated in detail to his wife, he requested her thus saying:

> In this way she cried (that her husband had instructed
> her to do so) so you too, at the side of my death bed
> do the same for me. This is what I'm telling you, what
> I want to say to you (Mihir Sangma, 1996, 49).

He completed the narration and died in his sleep. The story says, after his death, she did the same for her husband just the same way the bird cried for her husband. After this, it says that the *kabe* began to be used as a dirge among the *A·chiks* during the funeral ceremony (Mihir Sangma, 1996, 49).

Dirge is sung by the female members of the bereaved family, close relatives or professional mourners who take turn to sing. The funeral dirge is recital of merits of the departed, as well as a prayer for him/her to reach his/her goal without mishap. The stories of the deeds of valour and fame, or the pinnacle of glory reached by their sons and spouses are uttered (Wa·tre, 2007, 58-59). *Chitmang* or *Balmang*, an isolated hill in the South Garo Hills, is believed to be the home of the spirits of the dead. The song begins with the instructions to the deceased. The child is asked to make his way to the land of *Chitmang* and the waters of *Balmang*. He is told to rest and have his lunch at *Chidimak* - where the spirits bathe: "My fathers, for a little while sit, my bird, for a little while stand" (Caroline Marak, 1985, 60). The spirit of the child is asked to stop for a while in the resting place of the ghost *Bogia*, where *Chanapa*, a demon, sighed with relief after a steep climb. That is the place he must have his lunch after tethering the bull to the *boldak* tree (Schima Walichii). The spirit is cautioned that on its solitary journey it may encounter *nawang*, a demon which devours the souls of men on their way to *Chikmang*. To escape from *nawang*, the spirit must throw down his arm-rings and feathers, while the demon collects them the spirit gets a chance to run to safety. After this advice the child is compared to an umbrella shielding them from the elements, and to *Bolong* (Cyathocalyx martabanicus) and *sal* trees (Shorea robusta). The child is further compared to a young bull that is developing a hump and horns which the parents watch tenderly (Caroline Marak, 1985, 61). The mother bids the spirit to remember its home, so that at the time of reincarnation it may be born into the same family. The spirit must proceed cheerfully with eyes raised and a pleasant smile upon its lips.

The themes in *Kabe* are mostly of love, affection and an appreciation for the good life led by the deceased. In the post funeral ceremony *Kabe* the themes differ in the sense that they acquire a counseling nature, cautioning the spirit of the dangers that are to be expected from the malevolent *nawang*. They also wish the spirit a good life at *Balpakram*.

Traditionally through *kabe*, the *A·chiks* pray for a good after-life of the deceased in the land of the *Waimong*, the care taker of the land of the spirits. Traditionally it is believed that the relatives or the family members can lead the spirit of the deceased to a better life in the life after death through a soulful rendering of *kabe*. In other words, a meaningful recall of all the good deeds of the departed soul would perhaps help in winning some appreciation for the deceased in the land of the spirits. There are various *kabe* that are recited at different times;

3.5.2. *Kabe* for an uncle who is on his death bed

The song says that the death of the maternal uncle is a great loss for the *A·chiks* since he bore great responsibility in all family matters. Therefore, here the family members cry in great agony for the lost soul (Mihir Sangma, 1996, 89).

3.5.3. *Kabe* by the wife for her deceased husband

The *Kabe* says that the wife is going to face problems after the husband's death. She is afraid to face the difficulties and dangers in future and face life alone. The wife wails that there will be no one to repair the broken roof, no one to take shelter in when troubles vex the family, no one to work with, and no one to watch over the paddy field.

3.5.4. *Kabe* by the mother/maternal aunt for an uncle

The song speaks about the great loss. The mourners speak to the spirit (*mite* - mɪt͡ʃ-e) to receive the deceased and not be silent to their request.

3.5.5. *Kabe sung* at the mother's death

In the song at the mother's death the relatives and friends wail saying that there will be no one to take care of the children. The children will be like the chicks, motherless and crying for food and will be scattered about. There is no one like the mother to care for them lovingly and her death will be an irreparable loss.

Kabe contributes and reflects the rich cultural values of *A·chik* traditional society. It is an interesting feature of the *A·chik* society where mourners relive the memories of the deceased by recounting all the deeds and actions of the past in such appropriate selection of words that no one is able to ignore the gravity of the moment overflowing with tragedy.

3.6. *Doroa*

Doroa is kind of song sung mostly during *Wangala* festival, it is sung in praise of *Minimaa Kiri Rokkime*, the goddess of rice and about the origin of incense which is usually addressed to *Misi Saljong*, the god of blessing. *Doroa* is related to the myths of creation, and gives imaginative explanation of natural phenomenon. It relates to the history of the tribe, describes the land they came from, their leaders and manner of migration, origin of *chatchi* and *ma·chong*. *Doroa* embraces the customs and the ways of life as they had been for generations. This narrative is called *Ma·ambi* (Mignonette, 2003, 69). Other important aspects of life covered by *Doroa* are beliefs and mythology on which are based rituals and ceremonies. Myth and faith are inextricably woven together. Myths exist in the consciousness of the whole tribe. It is concerned with the creator and the different gods. It starts with the state of earth in the primordial period, and then proceeds to the creation of animate and inanimate objects, and the purpose of creation. It recalls how the creator invited all the living things to himself in the underworld to appraise each of its function, to reveal himself to them and teach them to celebrate the gift of life by dancing to the rhythm of musical instruments. To this all the gods and goddesses were also invited: *Misi Saljong* (god of blessings and distribution), *Susime* (god of wealth), *Minimaa Kiri Rokkime* (goddess of fertility), and each was apportioned a duty. It pointed out that only man was absent at this great festival. *Ase* and *Malja*, sent to represent mankind, failed to turn up at the function, hence *Ase* was killed by a tiger and *Malja* was taken by mermaid. Since then *Ase* and *Malja* have become symbols of disobedience to authority and to cosmic order.

According to tradition, it is said that *Noro Mande*, the first man did not know how to sing *Doroa*. But once the gods and goddesses quarreled over the death of *Dore* (a white headed babbler), and over the broken leg of a *bengbul* (frog) because they were the only two who knew how to sing *Doroa*. As there was none else left to sing *Doroa*, descendents of the gods and goddesses tried to sing it by moving their lips but they could not utter the words. So it was left to *Tatara Rabuga*, the Creator, to revive and refashion *Dore* and *Bengbul*. From the living beings of the earth and of the water, the 'prawn' went to the land of the gods and goddesses to take part in *Doroa* where he learnt the song for seven years and seven seasons in the underworld of gods and goddesses. After coming back from there, he demonstrated and taught others how to sing *Doroa*. Since then, a squirrel that lives on trees and a field cricket that makes hole on the ground imitated *Doroa* and demonstrated by making music with their hands on their mouths. Thus the first man *Noro Mande* started imitating it and began to sing *Doroa* (Harendra Marak, 2010, 88-89).

Doroa is basically a prayer offered to *Minimaa Kiri Rokkime*, the goddesses of rice, who lives in the underworld in the country beneath the waters of the great sea *Songduma - Rekbokchiga*. She is implored to come and make her abode in the *jhum* land by putting on her *gana* (woman's dress) and wearing *seng·ki* (waistband) on her hips. She is begged to bring a handful of rice which would be enough for one season (Harendra Marak, 2010, 82). A pig, a cock and an egg are offered to seek her blessings for a good harvest. The prayer also includes a request to bring along with her *na·ma* (the mother fish).

Doroa also tells about the cycle of cultivation, the rites and ceremonies conducted during a year; *a·galmaka*, *jumangsia*, *ja·megapa*, *rongchu-gala*, etc. Beliefs and myths associated with cultivation are also described, such as the origin of the mother of paddy, of various vegetables grown in the *jhum*, etc.

In poetry, such as *Doroa* and *Dani*, which narrates myths and the names of ancestors of numerous objects, like squirrels, monkeys and domestic fowls, we come across the *A·chik* concept of the earth and the world-view. Their answer to the basic questions of life, their belief in sacredness of life, belief in immortality of the soul and what happens in the afterlife may be obtained from certain myths.

Doroa does not merely bear religious value but also serves as the unwritten records about rituals and ceremonies and beliefs which are embedded in Traditional Oral Literature.

3.7. *Do·sia*

The principal form of marriage among the *A·chiks* is *Do·sia*. The meaning of this term is 'killing a fowl'. *Do·sia* simply refers to the *A·chik* traditional marriage. The *kamal* performs the ceremony invoking the gods to bless the couple. The bride takes the initiative to fetch the bridegroom. A cock and a hen, furnished by the girl's family must be sacrificed and eaten. Among the *A·kawes*, the priest holds the cock and the hen by the wings and holds them in the presence of contracting parties asking some questions, to which they reply *nama* (good). The priest then holds the fowls close together, and strikes them with a piece of wood. He then drops them to the ground. The fowls struggle a little before dying and their relative positions after death determines whether the omen is good or bad. If the heads of the birds lie with the beaks pointing towards each other, the omen is good, but if they lie with their beaks apart, it is bad (Playfair, 1998, 101).

Among the *am·bengs*, the manner of performing this ceremony is somewhat different. The *Kamal* takes the hen, and holding it by its legs or the wings, strikes the woman on the back with the hen, and at the same time repeats an incantation, which translated, runs as follows: "Certain ones have this day consulted the omen of the fowls. If they are to be bound to each other like the melon clings to its support, or the *setiri*, or the *badagong* (kinds of climbing cane), or the *re* (another kind of cane), then the hen will look to the man and the cock to the woman" (Playfair, 1998, 101). The man is treated in the same manner. The priest then holds the fowls together, and with one effort pulls off both heads and throws them on the ground. For the omen to be good, the beak of the cock should, as it lies on the ground, point towards the woman, and that of the hen towards the men.

The *do·sia* is followed by the *do·biknia* (another form of consulting the omens). An incision is made in the stomach of one of the birds, and the *kamal* draws out the larger intestines and holds them out before him. If they hang together, the omen is good but if they are apart, desertion or death is predicted. If the intestines are full of digested food, the couple will be rich and if empty, they will be poor (Playfair, 1998, 102).

3.8. The Narrative of Salling or *Katta Salling*

Regarding the narrative of *Salling* or *Katta Salling*, Caroline Marak observes that the theme of nature and the seasons, objects and forces of nature and the *jhum* field forms the subject of this narrative. In a way the song covers the whole panorama of *A·chik* rural life in the hills, noting the changes in nature caused by the cycle of seasons. The poem is divided into sections, each dealing with one season. A section of the poem presents not the static objects, but nature in continuous flux in the process of growth or decay under the influence of the elements. A phase in the life-cycle of nature is thus described in each section.

The first season of the year is the Windy Season, a period of hot and dry spell, which is accompanied by strong winds. The land is dry and the wind raises so much dust that the atmosphere is thick, obscuring vision. The second line conveys the sound of the splitting bamboo inter-knots, due to extreme dryness and heat. The brown cicada after the silence in winter once again fills the air with the sound *Siao-siao*. The poet then speaks of the effect of the hot sun on human beings.

> Atmospheric dust obscures vision,
> Inter-knots of bamboo split *tiptap-tiptap.*
> *Cicada* emits the sound *siao-siao*
> Sweltering heat produces burning sensation.
>   (qtd. in Caroline Marak, 1985, 64)

In the second season the poet describes how a great change comes with the onset of monsoon. The earth is covered by green vegetation. Various kinds of creepers, millet and bamboo shoots grow in *jhum* field. Green cicada and field cricket appear in this season. The young crabs leave the mother and the female fish swim upstream to eat the flowers of trees that fall into the water. Wagtails and bobolink sings. The fruits of *bolchim* (Duabanga sonnetatioides) form into small balls while *dimbil* (Careya arborea) bears tufts of hair like flowers (Caroline Marak, 1985, 65).

The season of millet follows. To protect the ripening millet from predators, a member of each family keeps watch in the *jhum* at night. The fruits of *chama* (Astocarpus chaplasha) and *gasampe* (a kind of tree with edible fruits) ripen. *Chenggari* (a kind of cicada) makes a chirping noise in the evening. In the streams, cockles crawl on rocks and big fishes glide gracefully in deep pools. Leeches infest the jungles and overgrown paths. Doves make nests to lay eggs and feed their young with millet grains and toucans with black and white feathers are seen flying (Caroline Marak, 1985, 65-66).

Rice matures and is harvested late in the fourth season. As rainstorm becomes less the plantain leaves open wide and glitter in the sun. The pods of sesame grow large and spring onion blooms. Sitting on the stem of the cotton bush the *gukchru* (a kind of green locust) makes noise resembling the sound of a spinning machine. *Gaanti* (a kind of cicada) fills the air with a ringing sound while the silk spider spreads its web along the pathway. *Gan·drak* (a kind of green frog) makes the sound *gak gak* on the waterfalls where it lives while the red squirrel cries *chak chak* close by the boundary of the *jhum* (Caroline Marak, 1985, 66).

In the fifth season the *me·gong* (Barebinia variegata) trees are covered with flowers and various kinds of tall grass also bloom in the cold season. *Kitma* (Rhus semialata) bears white berries and the bean of *abilik* (a genus of bean) becomes half ripe. The woodpecker strikes the *olmak* (sterculia villosa) while the porcupine gnaws pumpkin in the *jhum*. The fragrant *chaging* (a late variety of rice) is ready to be prepared into flattened rice. Streams become smaller; *na·chi* (a kind of fresh water fish) takes shelter in water source and bigger fishes in pools. *Do·aran* and *do·sisi* (kinds of bird) migrate into the plains. Rodents leave their holes and hollows of trees (Caroline Marak, 1985, 66-67).

3.9. *Katta Agana* or the Epic Story Narration

Katta Agana or the epic story narration consists of a vast, seemingly inexhaustible and number of poems on the legend of the *A·chik* heroes *Dikki* and *Bandi*. It appears to be one of the oldest form of oral literature of the *A·chiks*, immensely popular, is common to all the *A·chik* communities within the Garo Hills and outside, and known by different names in different regions.

In a way *Katta Agana* or the epic story narration is also a mirror of the unwritten history and culture of the *A·chiks*. It describes a land where mighty heroes and enchanting ladies lived, where the people were wise and where mighty deeds of valour occurred. The mighty deeds of heroes and heroines, manners, customs, ways of living and thinking, war and peace in the *A·chik* community make for the subject matter of the poem. Various stories are told of a host of characters, chief of who are *Dikki*, *Bandi* and *Balwa* (Caroline Marak, 1985, 68). They are the most famous brothers in the world. In the songs of *Katta Agana, Dikki* is always portrayed as an *A·chik* beau, ideal of a warrior-statesman, saint and philosopher. He is the mightiest spirit who ever appeared on the stage of the world's human history. He is a man of superlative vision, of exalted mind and of intense spiritual nature. He lives in close touch with the rulers of elements and the nature-spirit who govern natural phenomenon, all of whom are conscious intelligences. For this reason, he is also known as *Rurime Todik*, that is, the Heroic Spiritual Being. *Rurime Todik* is identified by most *Katta Agangipa* (narrator) with the Sun-Myth. He is often sung with praises by them to have received instructions from the Sun-God himself. True wisdom is a part of his being. He has a perfectly sound conception and thorough understanding of human race. *Dikki* is the wisest of the wise. *Bandi* is the strongest, the bravest and the most alert warrior in the world. *Balwa* is the fleetest and the finest looking man in the world.

3.9.1. *Dikki*

Dikki the central character of the song and the greatest legendary of the *A·chiks*, born and brought up in his mother's country, a place of great beauty and wealth, which is described as the most ideal, the most famous and the most glorious country in the world, which has never been conquered by any foreign foe since the beginning of time:

> The Heavenly Central Land
> The Child of *Salgra*, the God of Light,
> The Country of Silver pillars,
> Where bullions of gold are piled…
>   (qtd. in Rongmuthu, 2008, 19)

Peerless in physique, wisdom and strength, *Dikki* has completely subdued his basic instinct to noble spiritual ideals of high intellectual and spiritual order. Through his occult powers, *Dikki* can entrust his soul to his adopted mother, *A·ning Bokrinima Chining Randinima*, the goddess of energy and vitality in the underworld for safe keeping whenever he goes to battle. If his body is killed, his spirit flies to it and revives it. In times of sorrow his communion with the forms and powers provide him with joy. His contact with the invisible forces enables him to cause thunderstorms at will. His kind and sympathetic nature, and sagacity accounts for his popularity as a ruler. Though he is the leader of his people, his life is unostentatious and dedicated, like that of a sage, to the search for truth and to intellectual and spiritual advancement. Quiet and unobtrusive, service is his ideal. He believes in the sanctity of all things, animate and inanimate.

Dikki, thus emerges as the finest specimen among men. In the past he was held with pride and reverence as the ideal by the *A·chiks*. In his praise it is sung thus:

> His face is that of *Salgira*, the sun god;
> His body is that of *Moepa*, the resplendent sun;
> And his voice is that of *Goera*, the God of Thunder and Lightning.
>
> (qtd. in Caroline Marak, 1985, 70-71)

Under the wise rule of *Dikki*, his country attains prosperity and moral perfection. *Dikki* himself sets an example by personally clearing and cultivating the land, growing cereals and fruit trees. In this country labour is never a matter of servitude but of honour. *Dikki* is praised for his godlike strength, courage and other supernatural qualities. He is portrayed as a shining pillar of silver or a bar of gold, a demi-god and a man of great spiritual learning. Also as one who has been moulded along with *Dakdame*, the goddess of vitality and strength as well as *Rurime*, the goddess who moulds human forms (Wa·tre, 2007, 58).

Tales are woven around *Dikki*'s marriage to *Giting*, a girl said to be the hero's counterpart in qualities of head and heart. Some of the female characters in the song are *Dikki*'s younger cousin sisters who are virtuous, beautiful and share his occult powers. The images in this narrative give a Utopian description of the land of *Dikki* as a place which is so prosperous, that gold and silver coins are freely strewn in the village courtyard and where crops are so plentiful that they (the paddy and the banana flower) bend with the weight of their abundance. The symbolic image of the tree on which many different fruits of gold, silver, bananas, paddy, etc bloom in rich abundance.

Dikki has become a master of matter and of the nerves of men for high divine purpose beyond the comprehension of mere humanity, possessing powers which other human beings do not possess; but at the same time he lives as a perfect man of the world among his own people. He commands the universe and through his comprehensive fundamental knowledge of the wonderful field of matter, of the perspectives of the true nature of man, and of the varied degrees of human consciousness.

> *Dikki*, the shining pillar of lustrous silver,
> *Todik*, the glowing bar of gold;
> *Dikki*, the living demi-God,
> *Todik*, the occult-savant…
>   (Rongmuthu, 2008, 120)

The 'Epic Story Narration' may be described as an epic, because the narrative covers a vast subject, numerous places connected with the past history of the *A·chiks*, apparently unending adventures of the heroes, the legend of *Dikki*, his romance and the stories of his cousin sisters. It possesses solemnity of tone characteristic of an epic.

3.9.2. *Bandi*

Bandi and *Balwa* are the sons of *Dikki*'s maternal aunts. *Bandi*, like *Dikki*, is a perfect athlete, but quick tempered and scrupulous. *Balwa* (wind), true to his name, is the most nimble-footed of the trio.

Bandi is an extremely fine-looking warrior. He is the most ideal and has the most magnificent physique in the whole world. He is the finest specimen of human race. He has the most tremendous dynamic drive.

> Yonder, the Strong Warrior moulded of Pure Steel
> The dreaded Man-Eater, *Bandi* the wild swan.
> The Fierce-Looking Rapacious Hawk of the Sky…
>   (qtd. in Rongmuthu, 2008, 81)

In the battlefield, *Bandi* is seen to perfection. He is the finest, manliest, bravest and noblest of all warriors. In the midst of the bustle of battle, he is absolutely calm and cool. He is ubiquitous and his quick eyes see everything. Nothing fatigues him and nothing disturbs his equanimity. His intrepid heart is unmoved by the dangers into which his impetuosity leads him. No misfortune disconcerts him. His courage is indomitable, he displays unflinching determination and serene equanimity in the midst of noise and din of battle.

When victory is secured after the battle *Bandi* shouts hilariously in a high pitched thunderous voice:

> *Toban* (real warrior-hero) am I, a living image of *Goera*,
> The god of thunder and lightning
> The faces of rock-cliffs, as if they were mirrors,
> Bear living witness to my heroic deeds.
>   (Rongmuthu, 2008, 87)

3.9.3. *Balwa* or *Dingaraja Balwaracha*

Balwa, is a man of broad views and generous sympathies, intensely sensitive to oppression and wrong, filled with a passionate love of his countrymen and a desire to help them to nobler and higher national and social life. He gives his own countrymen the inspiration of a winsome personality possessing a spirit which can be used to leaven and uplift the world. In times of difficulties his is the spirit of fortitude, resilience, patience and tenacity. He is also a man of intense spiritual fervour. One cannot fail to understand that *Balwa*'s intense reverence for the Supreme Deity, known as *mite*, in whom he lives, moves and has his very being. He confesses himself overawed by the vastness of the Unknowable, appalled by the great vision of Everlasting Law, and silent in the contemplation of the infinite and the Eternal. His metaphysical acumen, versatile talents, pure patriotism and consistent piety have endeared him to all his countrymen. He possesses extraordinary human qualities of instantaneous reflex action, sound instinctive judgment of right lines of action, acute sense of personal grip on progressive plumes and courage. To his finest quality of brain he adds a sense of justice and honour. He is lovable, always calm, patient, generous, kind and humane.

In his home circle, he is an ideal husband and a devoted father. As a man of complete self mastery, he is never swayed by emotion of passion, but remains always believing in the loftiest possibilities. Oppression, cruelty, insincerity are hateful to him (Rongmuthu, 2008, 88- 93).

3.10. Folk Songs

Folk Songs are an intrinsic and inseparable part of the *A·chik* culture. Marked with diversity and versatility in composition and melody, songs remain ingrained in the day to day life of the *A·chik*s. The strength of the genre of the folk songs lies in their variety and flexibility, with each genre having a distinct identity of its own. The *A·chik*s weave tales of songs and songs of folk tales. People's beliefs, ritual ceremonies, agricultural activities, social functions, and love-life - all find expression in folk songs. Traditional *jhumming* practices have given birth to many folk songs. Merry making follows the ceremonial functions, which in turn leads to the composition or addition of new verses to the existing songs. Folk songs can be sung by ordinary people, whereas traditional sacrificial songs can be chanted or sung by a *kamal* (Rongmuthu, 1996, 63).

Folk songs are handed down by word of mouth from generation to generation. Spontaneity is evident in composition as it offers singers some leeway in adaptation and substitution of words in the songs. Its theme varies in range, with the creation of the earth at one end and love and romance at the other. The *A·chiks* lived and still lives in close proximity with nature and it is but natural that nature be a part of their legends, myths and folk songs. Original is the password for all the themes of the folk songs - origin of the earth, origin of the *Wangala* dance, courting through songs, love and romance, pure merriment, death of a loved one, emotions, expression of grief and so on. The *A·chiks* express their joys and sorrows, feelings and emotions, reflections of their way of life, zest for life, humour in life, fears, beliefs in gods and goddess, in things supernatural.

Folk Songs *Nanggorere, Gonda doka, Gogaia* and *Gosaia* may be taken as specimens of folk songs. Different types of imageries are used for different songs and some of the images are based on traditional customs, practices as well as beliefs and superstitious. Though all of them can be sung by one at any time and place, the young people specially like to sing them during leisure hours. The verses are sung alternately by young men and women singly or in chorus. All the folksongs are remarkable for their lyricism.

3.10.1. *Nanggore*

Nanggore is a song for all happy occasions, and the verses are sung alternately by young men and women singly or in chorus. However, there is no logical progression of thought from one verse to another because most verses are self-contained and are not continuations or replies to the previous ones. It is basically a love song that can be sung by anyone at any time and place, on any occasion except funeral. Though this song is romantic in nature, it also reflects the culture and tradition of the *A·chiks*. Moreover, the song is full of metaphorical languages in which a lover is often compared with the flora and fauna.

3.10.2. *Gonda Doka*

Gonda doka according to Dr. Julius L. R. Marak was started in the year 1922 -23. It is a song of nature and on human theme; the association also lies in the suggested choice of action. The verses may be sung alternately by young men and women. In every stanza of *Gonda doka*, the first line sung is about the nature and then the second line is on human deeds:

> Choose and transplant the best seedling of rice,
> Though my face and form are not comely, take me
> (as wife) out of love.
>   (qtd. in Caroline Marak, 1985, 75)

The two groups of young men and women join in singing the refrain which runs thus:

> Sing *Gonda*, Chant *Gonda*, I have twenty –six rupees
> on hand
> '*Dodoancheng, doancheng*' (a kind of bird) sweet heart,
> First draw me towards you.
>   (qtd. in Caroline Marak, 1985, 75)

The words 'twenty-six rupees' and *do·ancheng* are sung only for the sake of rhyme. The young man singing here obviously bids a particular young woman not to be jealous of another, who has won the heart of the young man she loved. The parallel points out that the maintenance of amicable relationship is as essential to life as the elements.

In *Atong* area the biggest festival is *Chugan* or post funeral ceremony. In earlier days the young man and young woman were not allowed to talk or communicate openly, the *Gonda doka* on several occasions serves to bring prospective lovers together. So through the *gonda* song they express their feelings towards each other when they meet for the first time. It is during *Chugan* or post funeral ceremony that the young men and women have freedom to choose their life partners. Through this song these young man and woman express their liking for one another and their willingness to start a friendship and sometimes it results in their elopement and marriage.

> I have already named you
> I have already made up my mind.
> When I am determined
> Can you decline (my proposal)?
>> (Caroline Marak, 1994, 46-47)

3.10.3. *Gogaia Gosaia*

Gogaia Gosaia may be sung solo or in chorus. It has a refrain which runs thus:

> *Gogai wai, gosai wai*
> *Direng wai.*

While this passage cannot be rendered into English, a verse will serve to illustrate the nature of the song:

> I, the brave, go along the plains, indeed,
> I go from village to village in order to challenge
> other men for a fight, indeed.
>   (qtd. in Caroline Marak, 1985, 76)

The reference is to the customary sport of the braves or warriors who go from one village to another offering a loin cloth to other braves, which is a gesture of challenging them for a fight. Anyone who accepts the offer accepts the challenge. Various aspects of *A·chik* customary life form the theme of *Gogaia, Gosaia*.

3.10.4. *Serejing*

Serejing is popular with the *A·chik* young men and women. There is more than one type of tune to this folk song. There are about six different tunes. Initially, the main theme was the flora and fauna, the streams, rivers and hills (Wa·tre, 2007, 48). According to Dr. J.L.R. Marak, the main theme of *Serejing ring·a* was a funeral wail or lamentation. On the death of her father and mother an *A·chik* lady named *Serejing* sadly lamented in the following way:

> Alas! I am alone without a mother or a father,
> Now I have to wander wretched and sad,
> I will look after the house and its surroundings
> And keep their memories alive
> Alas! Where else will I see my mother's face?
>   (qtd. in Julius Marak, 1999, 23)

There are no fixed rules for the creation of lyrics and the singer has the freedom to add his own creations, appropriately according to situations and circumstances. At times there is no linkage between the lines (Wa·tre, 2007, 48).

3.10.5. *Ahaoea* or *Ahaia*

Ahaoea or *Ahaia* is the song of the *Jamegapa* season, when the paddy has just been cut and is being brought into the granary. However, it can be sung throughout the harvest season, for it ushers in the time of feasting and merrymaking (Wa·tre, 2007, 38). Several *matta* (pointed digging sticks) are accumulated near the farm house at the field. The members of the household in the field take these *matta* and make ceremonial representation of some phase of cultivation after which the grains are neatly plucked and bounded in sheaves. The person who carries the *medong* (sheaves of paddy) in a bamboo basket comes shouting 'Ah, ha! ha! Mother of earth; Ah!ha! ha! Mother of food grains.' This kind of singing is called *Ahaoea* (Julius Marak, 2000, 68-69). Every evening boys and girls dance together to the accompaniment of drums, bamboo flutes and *adil* (trumpet made of buffalo horn). They enter each and every house with slow and swaying movement and singing the famous indigenous song *Ahaoea*. This is the song to exchange views and ideas and expressing one's love and gratitude as offering of the rice beer to the young drummers by the young dancing girls continues (Mihir Sangma, 1994, 48).

3.10.6. *Araowaka*

Araowaka, is a song for any occasion and has a lively, catchy tune. It is sung in the *Chisak* area of the Garo Hills. The refrain appears to be an imitation of some bird sound.

> The beautiful yellow blossom – *araowaka*
> Is the mustard flower – *araowaka*
> Though you live in another village – *araowaka*
> Please do not forget me – *araowaka*.
>   (Wa·tre, 2007, 45)

3.10.7. *Rere Ring·a*

Another indigenous romantic *A·chik* song called *Rere Ring·a* is sung by the three divisions of the *A·chiks*: the *Rugas*, the *Duals* and the *Chiboks*. It is sung on joyous occasion by the young people, through which they tease one other.

> Oh I mistook you for a chief
> Because of your umbrella
> Back home I'm sure
> You're as poor as me
> *Ha - re - re*
>   (Wa·tre, 2007, 46)

3.10.8. *Chera sola*

Chera sola is sung only in the *Gara-ganching* area. The subject of this particular song is usually the heroes and heroines of old like *Jingjang*, *Nongdu a·ding pante*, *Gangga* and *Rutha*, exchanging views and ideas as sometimes putting questions and answers of old tales (Mihir Sangma, 1994, 52). It is a traditional song and sung responsively by young man and woman and it can be sung anywhere.

> O dear! *Jingjang*'s country
> The land of *Nangal*
> Has seven hundred households
> And tens and thousands of children.
>   (Wa·tre, 2007, 50-51).

3.10.9. *Dime ring·a*

Dime ring·a is a specialty of the *Atong* area. It is sung after the *mangona* (post funeral) ceremony amidst dance, gaiety and music. It is called *Chugan* by the *atongs*. This particular song, however, is not confined to *mangona* only but can be sung at any time. Like the *Nanggorere* each verse of *Dime ring·a* consists of four lines with alternate rhymes. The response may be given by any member of the opposite group. The following song is sung by a young man.

> Whose sheaf of thatching is this?
> I shall pull off the thatching grass;
> Though I have a good view (of her village)
> I feel her absence deeply,
> (So) I shall run away with her.
>   (Wa·tre, 2007, 53)

There are many other folk songs, the above mentioned are just a few of the many that are found in Garo Hills. Different types of imageries are used for different folk songs and some of the images are based on traditional customs, practices, as well as beliefs and superstitions. Creative similes and metaphors have been utilized to express each and every imagination of their minds in the most beautiful way. In *The Traditional Dances of the Garos*, Dewansing Rongmuthu says:

> The genuine Garo folk songs, as handed down by tradition, are soul-stirring songs, full of romance, full of beauty and pathos, full of sentiments of love, life and death. They sing expressions on the eternal triangle in human affairs, on the sanctity and divinity of human life at its best and on the glimpses of divine substance in man. Some folk songs project out essentials for continued survival of human race. They are, in fact, the spontaneous expressions of the soul of the Garo race (Rongmuthu, 1996, 12).

Chapter IV

Myths and Archetypes in the Garo (*A·chik*) Folk Life

Myths and legends are traditional verbal materials passed on orally rather than in writing through generations. They form an essential part of the folklore of the people. The *A·chiks* have developed a rich store of folklore. The *A·chik* myths and archetypes are those connected with rivers and the physical features of the lands they settled in. Archetypes occur in different times and places in myth, literature, folklore and rituals. They have woven myths and archetypes around mystic and mysterious physical phenomena like that of the rivers, clouds, the thunder, lightning, the sun and stars, the hills and other natural formations to give plausible and imaginative explanations of their origin and existence, adding more mystery to them in the process. An element of reverence and fear can be traced in those myths. Myths make a large part of the thematic content of their oral narratives and poetry. Myths serve to explain the intentions and actions of supernatural beings. Most myths are concerned with religion, which involve rituals and prescribed forms of sacred ceremonies. A religious myth is the mental and spiritual orientation by which human beings relates themselves to the divine. The symbolism, the imagery and the rites of different people reflect their particular need in their life-situation and orientate them about its existence. Eliade would say:

> Religious symbols, inspite of their cultural differences, emerge from the human need to live in a paradigmatic world, to participate in the mode of being of gods and supernatural beings at the beginning of things (Dhavamony, 1973, 154).

Religious person realizes that this cosmos and the order of men emerge from the workings of the divine and supernatural beings. A significant way by which man expresses his religiosity is to live according to religious myth and ritual. Within religious context, myth and ritual are the dynamic power whose embodiment brings forth the sacred reality and makes the religious person live this reality in everyday existence. There is an intrinsic relationship between the divine power and its symbolic image. Man's existence is seen to be dependent on the sacred manifested in the symbols which are found in myths and rituals.

Some of the recurring myths that have a strong presence in the cultural narratives of the *A·chiks* are associated with places like *Balpakram*, rivers like *Songdu* (Brahmaputra), hills like *Dura A·bri*, *Rangira*, with spirits, mountains, with ideas of reincarnations, pools as in *Te·matchi Wari* (in river Ildek), *Mrik Wari* (in river Simsang), *Dombe Wari* and many more.

Psychoanalyst Carl Jung, in *Archetypes and the Collective Unconsciousness* (1968), illustrates the four types of archetypes. They are (i) mother archetypes, (ii) forms relating to rebirth, (iii) spirits and (iv) trickster figures. These archetypes of Jung can be traced in Garo (*A·chik*) folk narratives.

The concept of 'narrative' is often, explicitly or implicitly, tinged with connotations of 'fiction'. An emphasis on the plurality of stories is, among other things, a reaction against such concepts as 'truth', 'reality', 'theory', or 'validity in interpretation'. Power, rather than validity, is often seen as the factor informing choice among alternatives. In some social-political contexts, 'narrative' is seen as a way of giving voice to minorities or disadvantaged groups, generally repressed and silenced by the hegemony. These connotations of 'narrative' are particularly prominent in feminism, post-colonialism, legal studies, and the medical humanities. Although stories can give voice to individuals and groups that are often marginalized by the hegemony, they can also lose their political power by being interpreted as 'merely stories': as Kenan puts it "even when accounts remain rooted in a critique of hierarchy, storytelling has real dangers" (2006, 15).

Ryan says that a narrative is a sign with a signifier (discourse) and a signified (story, mental image, semantic representation). The signifier can have many different semiotic manifestations. It can consist for instance of a verbal act of story-telling (diegetic narration) or of gesture and dialogue performed by actors (mimetic or dramatic narration) (Ryan, 2001). The *A·chiks* have developed the act of story-telling to a large extend to communicate their myths and archetypes.

4.1. Mother Archetype

The mother archetype appears under an almost infinite variety of aspects. Mythology offers many variations of the mother archetype. The symbols of the mother in a figurative sense appear in things representing the goal of our longing for redemption, such as Paradise, the Kingdom of God, the Heavenly Jerusalem etc. Many things arousing devotion or feelings of awe, as for instance the Church,

University, city or country, heaven, earth, the woods, the sea, matter, even the underworld and the moon can also be mother-symbols. This archetype is often associated with things and places associated with fertility and fruitfulness. The qualities associated with it are maternal solicitude and sympathy; the magic authority of the female; the wisdom and spiritual exaltation that transcend reason; any helpful instinct or impulse; all that is benign, all that cherishes and sustains, that fosters growth and fertility (Jung, 1968, 82). In mythology, the mother archetype is often linked to the idea of the Great Mother. This includes Great Mother deities such as *Gaia* and Mother Earth. Rivers are among the earth's most vital resources. Much of human activity and development centres on rivers and bodies of water. Water is the beginning of life, it is also a principle of life, a primordial force that generates, vivifies and regenerates life. For *A·chiks* the river forms a major archetype and it symbolizes fertility as well as a mother figure.

One of the oldest symbols which date back to antiquity is the river. Apart from its practical utility as a commodity, the river has about it a mysterious, elusive and fascinating quality. This, coupled with the fluctuations of the tides has made it a perennial symbol of the ebb and flow of human fortunes (Gurudev, 2004, 137). Down the ages, water has been a symbol both of fertility and of resurrection. Centuries can be telescoped through the image of a flowing river (Gurudev, 2004, 139). A river is commonly associated with powerful feelings. Images of flooded rivers, overflowing its banks are analogues to human emotions like bursts of pent up fury, welling sorrow, drowning in a sea of pain etc (Gurudev, 2004, 141). Rivers have sometimes been considered the ultimate reservoirs of truth. It is the river that answers one's deepest questions.

The river forms a major theme in *A·chik* folk narrative mostly symbolizing fertility as well as motherhood. The Rivers are also shown as enduring symbols of the passage of time. It also highlights the conception of a river as the source of the origin, evolution and growth of human civilization. Kanak Chandra Sharma in his article writes: "The Brahmaputra in *A·chik* is called the *Songdu* river… They also call it *Amawari* meaning 'the mother of rivers'. *Songdu* represents the female aspect of a benign divinity." This is revealed in a folk story called 'Earthquake' found in *Apasong Agana* (As told by our Forefathers) compiled by Dewansing Rongmuthu. When the Supreme Goddess, *Nostu Nopantu* began fashioning the earth, rock and stone were made to grow into various shapes and sizes, thus making the earth stable; then the mother earth was cut into furrows. Into these newly fashioned furrows water freely flowed. The *A·chiks* called this accumulation of water, *Aema Ditema* or 'mother of fullness and overflowing', *Songduma, Sagalma* (mother of oceans) etc. In many folktales, the name *Songdu* occurs as the name of the river Brahmaputra. In the story *Durama Imbama, Simera*, the daughter of *Durama Imbama*, the tutelary Goddess of *A·chikland* in the *A·chik* Pantheon is married to *Singra*, the son of mother *Songdu* who is represented by the river *Songdu* (Kanak Chandra Sharma, 2004, 71).

There is a legend that the world was gradually created by a Goddess named *Nostu* who sprang up from a self begotten egg and from her womb streams of water issued which became rivers. After that all kinds of seeds and grass sprang up, then fish, birds and animals appeared and lastly but very significantly man came up. It highlights the conception that the river is the source or origin, of the evolution and growth of human civilization (Kanak Chandra Sharma, 2004, 74).

Caroline Marak is of the opinion that rivers are used predominantly as symbols in literature. Rivers, streams, mountains and rocks are full of archetypes and myths. The *A·chiks* believe that Garo Hills is a dwelling place of the gods and goddesses whom they worship. The *A·chiks* have always been fascinated by the rivers, streams and their sources. Much of their poetry, folklore and legends are connected with rivers. They have explored all such water bodies in the Garo Hills, and given them appropriate names, as also to their flora and fauna. Gods are believed to dwell in the rivers, their sources, in the forests and in the mountains. Rivers are their source of sustenance and well being (Caroline Marak, 2004, ix). The land, full of flora and fauna adorns the entire hills and mountains of Garo Hills and the people living therein. They keep alive the hills, mountains, valleys and make them suitable and pleasant to live in.

Garo Hills is blessed with rivers, lakes and streams making the land fertile, the naturally available items of food are found in abundance. In the early days people never went hungry because they knew how to use nature and live with it (Julius Marak, 2004, 154).

Earlier *A·chik* villages were located near some stream or waterfalls. Kanak Chandra Sharma observed that the *A·chiks* were great lovers of clean water. Water from streams and high waterfalls was piped through bamboo pipes to their places of residence. The fact remains that the river-system has remained a perennial source of benefit in various ways (Kanak Chandra Sharma, 2004, 75).

Most of the rivers of the District originate from the Tura and *Arbella* range, the centre and heart of the district, and the water dividing line or watershed falls through the centre from the West till it touches the Khasi Hills in the

East. Thereafter, the water divides, or the drainage basin of the district can be divided distinctly into two zones:

The Northern river basin zone

The Southern river basin zone

The Northern river basin zone can be demarcated into eleven sub river basins. The longest basin is *Damring* river and its tributaries and there are six large sub-basins, namely *Didram, Manda, Galwang, Ringgi, Didak*, and *Diti*. The rest of the rivers have only small basins. In the southern river basins, *Simsang* is the largest out of a total of fourteen rivers. The other river basins are *Ganol, Bugi, Darang* and *Bandra* and the rest are small rivers and streams only (Gassah, 1984, 26).

Goswami opines that there are a number of rivers and rivulets in Garo Hills with which several myths and tales are associated. The rivers in Garo Hills flow in three directions, that is, towards the north, west and south. The rivers *Damring, Ildek, Manda, Didak, Jinjiram, Didram* flow north while the *Ringge, Galwang*, and *Ganol* flow west and *Moheskhola, Mahadeo, Simsang, Dareng* or *Nitai, Bhogia* or *Bugi* flow down south. There are a few small rivers such as *Tulong, Marsi, Sonai, Roki*, etc. which flow westward. All these rivers have made remarkable contribution to the maintenance of good climatic condition in the Garo Hills for the preservation of its forest, growth of sal trees, bamboo forests, various types of decorative orchids, a large number of medicinal herbs, forest plants with food value and a good number of rare wild animals, birds, reptiles and fish, etc (Goswami, 2004, 101 - 102).

There are more than eight principal rivers in the district says Kanak Chandra Sharma that rise from the *Arbella* range and flow north – westward and namely the rivers such as *Dudhnoi*, *Krishnai* and *Jinary*. The river *Kalu*, known as *Ganol* rises near Tura and flows north-westward passing through *Goalpara* for about 16 kms where it finally falls into river *Jinjiram*. *Rongkhon* is the principal tributary of the *Ganol* river (Kanak Chandra Sharma, 2004, 75).

4.1.1. The Simsang or Someswari River

The *SIMSANG* or *SOMESWARI* rising from the *Nokrek* and taking a zigzag course enters the *Mymensingh* district of Bangladesh and falls into the *Kangsa* river (Kanak Chandra Sharma, 2004, 75). In olden times, the *Simsang* river was called *Chima* (*Chi*-Water and *Ma* - Mother). The *Simsang* is the largest and the second longest river in Garo Hills. D.N Majumdar wrote on this longest and largest river *Simsang*: "The *Someswari* flows through picturesque valleys, flanked with hills. In its upper reaches there are many waterfalls. One who has seen its crystal clear water and the carved pillar like stones along the banks can never forget it" (Kanak Chandra Sharma, 2004, 79). So this river was supposed to be the mother of all the rivers of the District. In connection with this, there is an old village known as *Chimagre* on the banks of this river named after the *Chima* river near *Nengkra* village (Mihir Sangma, 2004, 161**).** The banks of the *Simsang* river is also a treasure house of wealth and possession which is reflected in another story of *A·chik lore*, called *Kalkame Kalgra* (the god of destiny). In this story, *Durama Imbama*, the goddess of wealth and possessions, settled down in the *Simsang Rikam Rongdong Bra*, that is, the bank of the *Simsang* river at the confluence of the *Rongdong* stream on the eastern extremity of the Tura Range (Kanak Chandra Sharma, 2004, 80). The river offers vast scopes and possibilities for economic development of the region. The important tributaries of the *Simsang* river are *Rongkai*, *Rompa* and *Chibok*.

In the south-eastern region, the *Simsang* group of rivers has played a very prominent role in shaping the social and cultural life of the *A·chik* people.

4.1.1.1. The *Kanchru Wari*

The *Kanchru Wari* the literal meaning of which is the pool of the earthworm is immediately above the *Rangram Patal*. This is believed by the *A·chiks* to be the deepest pool in the *Simsang* river in the Garo Hills and, to be the headquarters of all the aquatic living beings. Aquatic serpents of immense size, known as *Sangknis* (sea serpents), are said to have made this pool their chief permanent abode. The *A·chiks* assert that there are enormous aquatic serpents, measuring between two hundred fifty to three hundred cubits in length in big rivers, pools and lakes.

These water bodies gain their impressive length and depth from the serpents that live in these *waris* (pools). These gigantic serpents are so afraid of *Goera*, the god of thunder and lightning, that they are seldom seen above the water (see Rongmuthu, 2008, 351).

4.1.1.2. The *Mrik Wari*

The *Mrik Wari* is in the *Simsang* river at *Rongbinggiri* which is believed by the *A·chiks* to be the second deepest pool in the *Simsang* river. The rocks on both sides of the pool, though rough shaped, are smooth surfaced and provide excellent seats to laze in. This pool is stated to be the *Chigat* or watering place of *Nokma Abong Chirepa*, the last independent and Paramount Highland Chieftain in the Hills, who had his headquarters on the left bank of the northern spur overlooking this pool. When the water is clear, this pool and the jagged rock on its banks look really grand. It is an excellent pool for angling (Rongmuthu, 2008, 310).

4.1.1.3. *Dengreng Kitik Wari Chora*

A deep eddying pool in the *Simsang* river, known as *Dengreng Kitik Wari Chora*, is sacred to the *A·chiks*. An ancient *A·chik* legend maintains that *Dengreng Kitik Wari Chora* was the *chigat* (watering place) of *Dimrimpa Dimsimpa Gaeripa Singeripa*, the ancient patriarch of *Mande* (man), who was the first to taste death among humankind (Rongmuthu, 2008, 336).

4.1.1.4. *Matma Wari*

Matma Wari or the pool of *Matma* (Buffalo) in the *Simsang* river beside the village of *Chimagre* in the mid-eastern part of Garo Hills is renowned among the *A·chiks* as the original and the first *chigat* (watering-place) of *Abong Noga Raja*, the Paramount *A·chik* Sovereign of all the Hills, now known as Garo Hills (Rongmuthu, 2008, 337).

4.1.1.5. The *Nosari Bandari Wari*

The *Nosari Bandari Wari* or the pool of *Nosari Bandari* in the *Bugi* river, on the south-eastern side of the *Nokrek* Peak of the Tura Range, is one of the most beautiful waterfalls in *A·chikland*. It is surrounded on both banks by rock-cliffs. According to an *A·chik* legend *Nosari Bandari* was once the abode of two water nymphs, named *Nosari* and *Bandari* respectively, who lived in friendly terms with the *A·chik* people. Certain signs of their habitation are said to be still visible by the pool (Rongmuthu, 2008, 337). According to an ancient legend of the *A·chiks*, *Gonga* (who first taught the *A·chiks* to make thread for clothing) is said to have spent many of his most romantic days here with his two lovers, catching fish, crabs and prawns, and bathing and swimming in the pool. *A·chiks* believe that the *Kilbolma* (gigantic cotton tree), which *Gonga* felled with the help of the god of the Winds, *Jaru Me·a Jabal Pante Okkuangsi Ja·patchongsi*, the god of winds, had grown by the side of this pool, some of its fossilized roots are still seen there (Rongmuthu, 2008, 312-13).

4.1.2. Damring River

The story of *Chela Asanpa* and *Brara* originated in a village on the banks of the *Damring* river. Similarly, in another folk story, about the Living Beings who 'First Acquired Steel', it is said that *Dakgipa Rugipa Tatara Rabuga* (literally, the Creator and the maker, the moulder, the most worshipped, the most profoundly taken), the supreme deity in the *A·chik* pantheon, fetched steel from the subterranean region for fire and the defense of humankind and melted it at a place known as *Chiginap Rongjamdap Chibrasni Chongsni*, that is, place of the confluence of seven streams of water where seven clumps of *Jati* bamboo grew. Rongmuthu in his book, *Folktales of the Garos*, mentioned that there was a place bearing these names, sacred to *A·chik* priests at the vicinity of the village *Rongribo* and *Kalak* on the upper reaches of the *Damring* river which flowed in the mid-northern part of the Garo Hills. For some other reasons also, the devoted *kamal* (priests) were said to be very respectful of this sacred place. Some *A·chiks* used to associate this place with the name of *Rama Cholsni*, that is, the parting of seven path ways. The bringing of steel is very significant, considering this as an important factor for the growth of civilization. For primitive people too fire and steel were the primary resources for leading a social life (Kanak Chandra Sharma, 2004, 77).

Dewansing Rongmuthu writes that the place is called *Chondodenga* Hillock in *A·chik* (1377 ft. high), lying east of *Mahadeo* river. It is also called *Ringchanchok*, meaning the 'leaning boat'. According to *A·chik* legends, in the past this hillock was on the seashore. A demigod, *Ago-Dinggopa*, followed by *Chando*, a merchant-prince, was bringing a boat laden with untold riches and treasures for *Dikki*, the renowned hero of *A·chiklore*. This boat is said to have capsized in this place. This hillock therefore contains within its bowels invaluable treasures which are being guarded by the theophanic spirit of *Chando*, the merchant prince (Rongmuthu, 2008, 326).

4.1.2.1. *Rongdik* River

The river *Rongdik* rises in the south-eastern side of the *Meminram* Peak of the Tura Range. A tributary of *Simsang*, it is mentioned in the *A·chik folktales* of *Dombewari*. The main incident of meeting the celestial damsel, *Opsora*[19]

---

[19]   The *A·chiks* believe that *Opsoras* or mitdemechiks (goddesses) are perfectly human in forms and features and dressed in snow-white clothes. They are reputed to be bewithchingly beautiful

or *mitdemechik* (goddesses) by the young *A·chikman Daran* occurred on the bank of the hill stream, *Chibok* flowing through the village, *Dingrang Bawegiri* (Rongmuthu, 2008, 46-53). Thus, it can be seen that most of the rivers in the Garo Hills, are linked with traditional stories and folklore.

4.1.2.2. *Dudhnoi* River

In Garo Hills, the river *Dudhnoi* is also called *Manda*. It originates from *Jangekoknal Damal* area of East Garo Hills and enters Goalpara and finally merges with the Brahmaputra. The region has no town and density of population is also low (Goswami, 2004, 103). The *Manda* river is nature's precious gift that has become an integral part of peoples' lives.

4.1.2.3. *Nitai* River

The *Nitai* is known as *Dareng* by the *A·chiks*. It also originates from the majestic *Nokrek* range in central Garo Hills. Flowing southwards it enters the *Mymensingh* district of Bangladesh, where it meets the *Meghna* River which ultimately pours into the Bay of Bengal. In the upper reaches, close to its source, the *Dareng* is lined with a rich tropical forest which is home to many wildlife species both flora and fauna. Besides watering the soil, the river adds

---

and capable of seducing young men by means of their charms. The *A·chiks* believe that the Opsoras are fond of bathing in lonely crystal clear pools or lakes, especially on top of high hills, during cloudless summer days. *Opsoras* are also believed by the *A·chiks* to be immortal beings.

moisture to the air through evaporation. Delicate ferns and rare orchids thrive in its moist conditions. Many of the deep pools, locally called *waris*, are surrounded by thick vegetation and rocky cliffs (Jacqueline Marak, 2004, 95).

Many of these *waris* are shrouded with myths and beliefs. It is believed that the *Redingsi wari* is the abode of a spirit with seven hands and seven eyes. People are forbidden to throw stones into the pool for fear of disturbing the spirit (Jacqueline Marak, 2004, 95). The *Redengsi wari* in the *Khakhija* Stream, one of the deepest pools and an important tributary of the *Dareng* river, is in the southern foot of the *Meminram* Peak of the *Dura* Range. It is one of the deepest pools in Garo Hills. A huge freshwater whale, having a large brilliant diamond on its head, is said to be living in the depth of this pool (Rongmuthu, 2008, 312).

4.1.2.4. *Ildek* River

The *Ildek* river is located in the East Garo Hills district. It originates from *Wa·ge Marang* near Papera Hill, bordering Khasi Hills, falling on the *Me·gam* area. The gorgeous *Ildek* river, where the gods and goddesses lived, flows majestically and winds its way through the high mountains towards the north of Garo Hills and enters Assam through Goalpara finally joining the mighty *Brahmaputra* or *Amawari*. The *Ildek* river is considered to be a sacred river for both the *A·chiks* and the non - tribals (Julius Marak, 2004, 154-55).

The *Ildek* river is perennial and not seasonal. It has contributed greatly to the economic activity of the people of the area. The river belt is fertile and the people cultivate it for their sustenance. Besides wet cultivation people also cultivate some vegetables and cash crops either for their own consumption or for selling the surplus in the market.

This river can also be utilized for transporting the products that cannot be transported through land. Thus cut bamboos, timber, jackfruits, pine-apples, etc. are transported to Assam by the people of Garo Hills through this river. The river can be used for transporting products throughout the season (Julius Marak, 2004, 157).

The *Ildek* river serves as a source of income during the dry season. There are plenty of fish in the river. The river not only serves the people but it also serves the animals. The *A·chiks* who practice traditional indigenous religion consider the *Ildek* river as sacred and holy because of its economic contribution to the people and because of the mythological important places that are found. The water is fresh and pure and the people try to keep it free from pollution.

4.1.2.5. *Anang Wari*

Anang Wari is in the *Ildek* river, in the north-eastern part of Garo Hills. It is a deep pool surrounded by cliffs. Many deities are believed to have lived in this river. The most powerful deities to live in this river are *Anang* and *Dilkang*. While walking or going along the river bank one should not utter the name of these two deities lest something happens (Julius Marak, 2004, 158). The river has three parts: *Anang Nokpante*, *Anang Nokmong* and *Anang Demechik*. All these pools are deep, *Anang Nokmong* being the deepest, having a depth of 40 ft. According to the divers there is a tunnel inside the *wari*. It is said that only a person who can dive up to 38/39 ft. can see the opening of the tunnel. Unlike the other *waris*, *Anang wari* is the widest and every year it gets silted with sand and at such times the opening of the underwater tunnel gets blocked. The water inside the tunnel is blackish in colour and it takes three poles of *wa·dro* (a kind of bamboo), each 8 ft. long joined lengthwise to catch the electric eel living inside. Whenever, someone dived, they used *dikge* (a tuberous herb of medicinal value of the order of the ginger and turmeric) to protect them from electric eel and other dangers (Fameline Marak, 2004, 192).

In the ancient days, three legendary heroes, *Anang*, *Dilkang* and *Dura* migrated from *Salaram Mitechak* (the divine Sanctuary of the East) and before settling down in this area, they consulted the divine oracle by *do·chi goa* (breaking eggs). The sign of the oracle did not favour *Dura,* who then left that place and went to the south central region to settle. Hence, we have the name *Tura* derived from *Dura.* However, *Anang* and *Dilkang* stayed back as the oracle sign favoured them. *Dilkang* went upstream and *Anang* stayed downstream (Fameline Marak, 2004, 192).

In the olden days the *A·chiks* dreaded this pool believing it to be the abode of a god *Anang,* and his brother *Dilkang* who used to cause insanity or madness among humankind. It was also believed by the *A·chiks* that *Gonga* (weaver and spinner) (Rongmuthu, 2008, 277) had thrown into this pool the anvil and hammer of the goddess *Dakgipa Rugipa Dingipa Babra* (Rongmuthu, 2008, 319).

Rivers and streams are priceless gifts of God to man. The beauty and usefulness of rivers has always inspired the imagination of man to weave countless myths, legends and folktales all over the world. Various kinds of legendary and mythical stories abound in the pools formed within the riverine course of *Ildek* in certain pockets. These deep and wide pools called *wari* have their own stories behind their original names, either mythical or legendary, though formed due to its natural course as it flows meandering through the hills, valleys and thick forests. The beliefs in the *waris* or deep pools of the *Ildek* river have greatly influenced the cultural practices of the different villages along the banks of the river (Fameline Marak, 2004, 187- 188).

4.1.2.6. *Malcheng Wari*

Malcheng Wari is the biggest and the most famous *wari*. Many stories are connected to it. The myth of this *wari* is that if a sacrificial offering of animals and fowl is made at this *wari* then the *A·chiks* believe it would propitiate their gods at the time of *A·galmaka* (ceremony immediately after the burning of debris for shifting cultivation and before planting seeds), at harvest time and in sickness, etc. There is also a myth that *Abet-Rangge* made his abode in this *wari* especially in the capacity of a god of nature.

The name of this *wari* came from a legendary figure called *Malcheng* who in ancient days, used to cross this *wari* and practiced shifting cultivation on the other side of the river. As the story goes, there was a python, which acted as a bridge across the *wari* and allowed *Malcheng* to cross over the river on its back. This went on for some time. A river mermaid, fell in love with *Malcheng* at first sight, and noticed his trips across the river. Determined to get him by all means, she requested the python to bring *Malcheng* to her. So, one day, while *Malcheng* was crossing the *wari*, the python took him on his back and sank down to the mermaid. The mermaid was very happy and married *Malcheng* and kept him with her for seven years. Thus, this *wari* came to be known as *Malcheng wari* (Fameline Marak, 2004, 188).

4.1.2.7. *Te·dambil Gure Simram*

Te·dambil Gure Simram is located beside the *Te·dambil* village on the banks of the *Ildek* river. There is a *ghat* or river bank used by the *A·chiks* who practice the indigenous religion to immerse the image of *gure mite* (a horse), which they worship. The horse god is believed to bestow wealth on whoever worships it and propitiates it with offerings of animals and fowl, but failing to do so may also invite wrath. The worshippers make the horse god idol out of bamboo splits and take it around the village in procession, after which they immersed it in the river. This particular bank of the *wari* was the immersion spot for their idol and so it came to be known as *Gure Simram* (*Gure* -horse, *simram* -immersion place).

4.1.2.8. *Rongjaleng Wari*

Three streams namely *Jajil chiring*, *Imbeng chiring*, *Rongkingkang chiring* (*chiring* - stream) meet together and drains into the *Ildek* river at *Aruak* village. During the dry season when the depth of the *wari* becomes shallow the protruding stone or *rongjaleng* across the river acts as a bridge enabling people to cross to and fro. People believe that there is a *Ku·gri mite* (*ku·gri* - dumb, *mite* -god) in this *wari* and this particular god has the power to make anyone dumb if it casts a spell. Of these three streams flowing into the *Ildek* river, *Rongkingkang* is famous for its natural endowments. This particular stream is strewn with many stones and boulders which seem to be stacked one over another (Fameline Marak, 2004, 189-190).

4.1.2.9. *Kimde Wari*

Kimde wari or the pool of the *Kimde* tree (Mesua ferrea) is also known as *Kimdegong wari*. An ancient *A·chik* legend states that in the ancient days, the *Kimde wari* was a very deep dark pool of water, reputed to be the home of huge black water-serpents, known as *sangknis* (sea serpents), and that, having shifted from their last homes at *Rongro Rongkimjeng Chiancheng Dasreng* on the north banks of the *Ildek* river. The lordly forebears of a once strong and warlike clan called the *Rongmuthu chatchi* (clan) settled by the side of the *Kimde wari* and to its west on the top of the *Weram Jambil* Hill. Large *Kimde* trees were then grown in abundance round about the *Kimde wari* (Rongmuthu, 2008, 338).

4.1.3. The Kalu River

The *Kalu* river is called *Ganol* by the *A·chiks*. Originating in the Tura range near Tura, it flows westwards in the Garo Hills and enters the Goalpara district of Assam. In the rainy season it is navigable only between the villages of Harigaon and Damalgiri (Goswami, 2004, 102).

Describing the *Ganol*, as one of the largest rivers in the Garo Hills, Carvel Marak says that it had a considerable role in shaping the socio-cultural life of the people living in and around the watershed in particular, and the entire Garo Hills in general. Originating in the central part of Garo Hills, it meanders westward down the hills and plains and joins the *Jinjiram* river, a tributary of the Brahmaputra river, at Mankachar in Assam near the Indo-Bangladesh border (Carvel R Marak, 2004, 59).

The *Ganol* watershed is of considerable importance because of its strategic location in the extreme west of the

State. Its physical features are characterized by steep slopes on the west of the *Nokrek* and Tura Hills, and narrow valleys along the river and its tributaries as it flows westwards. The area is covered by dense forests, wherever *jhum* farming and plantations are not practiced (Carvel R Marak, 2004, 59).

It is famous for its abundance of nature's gifts of flora and fauna. Some areas, especially at the source of the *Ganol* river adjoining the *Nokrek* Peak, are still covered with dense virgin forests. The area also abounds in traditional *A·chik* folk medicinal plants of which about two hundred plants have been ascertained.

The watershed of *Ganol* has also been supporting veritable human settlements for centuries. The fertile valley in the lower course of the *Ganol* along the foothills of the *Ranggira* range extend from *Damalgre* as far as the western border of Garo Hills and from *Me·lim* to *Goramara - Misikona* along the course of the *Ringgi* and *Dilni*, tributaries of the river *Ganol* and they constitute nature's bounty in the watershed. Permanent wet cultivation is practiced in these areas of the valley (Carvel R Marak, 2004, 64). Deep pools of the river are usually flanked by huge boulders which can provide shelter and protection to various aquatic lives especially during the dry season (Carvel R Marak, 2004, 66).

4.2. Forms relating to Rebirth

The concept of **rebirth** forms the second category of archetype which has various aspects, and is not always used in the same sense. Jung enumerates five different forms of rebirth namely: **Metempsychosis or transmigration** of souls; **Reincarnations, Resurrection**; **Rebirth** (Renovatio) and **Transformation** (Jung, 1968, 113-115).

4.2.1. *Balpakram*

In *Balpakram: The Land of the Spirits (Garo Mythology)*, Julius R. Marak affirms that the *A·chiks* have a strong belief in the Kingdom of God. The *A·chiks* believed that in *Chitmang* Hill lived a god almighty who was the giver of human lives. This god almighty can give life to human beings and cause death to human beings. This god almighty is known as *Waimong* by the *Atongs*. *Chitmang* hill is the *Me·mang Bugini Ja·nengtakram* and *Katchini Janepani Kasperam* (resting place of Spirit of *Bugi* and *Katchi-Janepa*). The *Chitmang* Hill is also known as *Waimong* (great deity). The *A·chiks* call the *Chitmang* Hill also as *Chitmang-Tangring-Rema-Bangjang*. *Goera*, the god of thunder and lightning, as well as the god of health and strength, was born in this place. Hence *Chitmang* Hill is a sacred hill for the *A·chiks*. In ancient days, when any unnatural calamities or sorrows befell the *A·chiks*, our great ancestors, would face towards *Chitmang* hill and pray saying, "Grandmother *Norimbi -Dikkimbi* save us from sorrow, grandmother look after us, care for us and defend us from all dangers" (Julius Marak, 2000, 61- 62).

It is believed that the spirit of the dead goes through *Chitmang* and then reaches *Balpakram* Hill. The *Chitmang* Hill is considered as the land of happiness being the resting place for the spirits of the dead. After living there for some time, one will be reborn again in one's own family. Evil persons are reborn as animals. It is the common belief of the *A·chiks* that the souls of those who commit suicide will not go to *Chitmang* and *Balpakram* but will go to the *Nokrek* Hill. Thus, *Chitmang* Hill becomes the place of happiness and joy to the *A·chik* indigenous believers (Julius Marak, 2000, 67).

They also believe that the original dwelling place of the spirits of the dead was *Napak*. Legend has it that since the day the spirits of the dead had found their new abode somewhere in the hills of *Balpakram*, the souls of all men started their journey (Julius Marak, 2000, 37). *Balpakram* Hill is also known as *Mangru-Mangram A·song* or *More-A·song-Mode-Chiga. Mangru-Mangram-A·song* or *More A·song-Mode-Chiga* means the land of spirits of the dead, a name given by the *A·chiks* for *Balpakram. Balpakram* is now to be the new abode of the spirits of the dead after migration from their original dwelling place *Napak* (Julius Marak, 2000, 65).

Playfair states that the *A·chiks*' beliefs on the subject of death and the after-life are among the most interesting of their many beliefs. Their funeral ceremonies are both varied and elaborate. It is believed that in the human body there lives a spirit, which on being released from its mortal covering, wends its way to *Mangru-Mangram*, the abode of the spirits, to reside for a period of time before being re-incarnated. The spirits are said to have first taken up their abode at *Napak*, a place in the north-eastern hills between *Damra* and *Cheran*. Later, when their numbers increased, they went to two hills, named *Balsiri Balpakram*, and they now wend their way to *Chitmang*, an isolated peak in the south-east region of the Garo Hills, not far from the *Simsang* river. *Mangru -Mangram* is a kind of purgatory through which all must pass, good and the bad alike. The journey to this place is a long one, and the spirit is provided with a guide, the necessary eatables and money as if he were about to set out on a long journey on earth. These requirements are provided by the sacrifice of the necessary animals, and the offering of food and liquor at the shrines which form the last resting-place of the deceased (Playfair, 1998, 102-103).

4.2.2. *Do·uang*

Some *A·chiks* believe that the common night-jar, *Do·uang*, is believed to be the messenger of news to the relatives of the deceased informing that it has seen his spirit on the way to *Chitmang*. It is most inauspicious for a night-jar to perch on the roof of a house, when this happens; the death of one of its inmates is thought to be imminent. If one of them is lying ill in the house at the time, it is believed that the bird has come to give the message that it is time for the soul of the sick man to start on its long journey (Playfair, 1998, 103). Their journey to this hill however, is not an easy one. It is said to be tiresome and torturous as the ghosts have to cross numerous hills, lakes, streams and bridges before they reach their final abode. They will have to travel with their heavy load on their backs, as it is custom of the *A·chiks* to kill the cow, put all their garments, food and their belongings along with the dead. The spirit of the dead would carry all the materials given to them in a *kera* (bakset) and take the cow and proceed towards their permanent abode (Julius Marak, 2000, 65).

4.2.3. Journey to *Chitmang*

On its way to *Chitmang*, the spirit is by no means free from danger, for at one place, there is the monster, *Nawang*, lying in wait. He accosts each spirit and demands what it has done on earth, and what property it has brought with it. The demon is covetous of brass earrings, and the spirit which is well supplied with these, throws them on the ground and escapes while the monster is engaged in picking them up. This in theory is the reason why men and women wear bunches of rings in their ears, though in practice, they are looked upon merely as ornaments, the myth being known to very few. Having arrived at *Mangru-Mangram*, the spirits reside there for a period of time until the appointed hour arrives for reincarnation (Playfair, 1998, 103-104).

On their journey, the spirits rest at a pool of water called *Me·mang Mesal Cha·ram -Chidimak Chikong* (the place for the spirits to eat their midday meal or the ink-water pool). Here they would refresh themselves and eat the food which had been sent with them and tether the bull which was killed for the dead to a *boldak* tree (schima walichii) (Julius Marak, 2000, 41).

The god of death comes to fetch every soul before its death and takes him or her to the place of spirits. The king of death is known as *Waimong. Wai* means the king of the spirits; *Mong* means more important than all the other spirits. The spirit or the soul of the dead person is being sent off, so that it might reach its destination. It is also believed that the king of death cannot receive the spirits of the dead into the home of the spirits unless the *Mangona* or *Chugan*[20] (post funeral ceremony) ceremony is performed before sending the spirits off. Otherwise, he would only be regarded as a sinner, his reward will be in the lowest form of reincarnation, and then such spirits remain simply in the form of spirits. The main objective of the ceremonial function is to send off the spirit of the dead person so that

---

[20]   The term and the ceremony of *mangona*, as myths show have an ancient origin. Even now, the word *mang* is used for a dead body, in preference to *manggisi* which means a dead body. Tradition, myth and religion are inseparably intermingled in the practice as in many others. This commemorative festival is also known as *Chugan Ringa* because a large amout of rice beer (*Chugan* in Atong) is used.

it might reach its final destination, the home of the spirits. Only then, will it be received by the king of death and be allowed to settle there at a suitable place. And through re-incarnation return to the virtuous life according to the dictates of the king of death (Mihir Sangma, 1994, 50).

The soul of a person does not perish along with the dead body. The soul remains and begins the process of forming a new flesh and body or enters another form of life in the process of re-incarnation. There are two different traditional practices among the *A·chiks*. The spirit of the dead person is said to be just sent off at the time of cremation, as the *Am·beng* and *Matabeng* do and this practice is known as *Watpaka*. The other one is to keep the spirit at home generally for a year until the next harvesting season which will then be observed as a sending off ceremony. This is known as *Mangona* and the process of keeping the spirit at home is called *Memang Ra·rika* (Mihir Sangma, 1994, 50).

At the time of the sending-off, the spirit of a child is compared to an umbrella which shields them from the elements, and also to *Bolong* and *Sal* trees. The child is further compared to a young bull as one who is powerful, strong and resourceful and can defend the family from all harm and danger or from the storms of life. The mother bids the spirit to remember its home, so that at the time of reincarnation it may be born into the same family. The spirit must proceed cheerfully with eyes raised and a pleasant smile upon its lips.

Robbins Burling says that *A·chiks* also display uncertainty as to the fate of the soul after death. It does seem that the mode of death affects the destiny of the soul, for those who die unnaturally in an accident or from an unusual disease, or who are killed by a wild animal, have difficulty in reaching the country of the dead; thus they may stay to haunt the place where they die, apparently as something of a grudge against those who are still living. Even those who die a natural death must undergo a perilous journey to get to the land of the dead (Julius Marak, 2000, 67). Side by side with this concept of an after-world is the belief that the soul can somehow be born again into this world, and even into the same family. A soul occasionally deserts a man's body and enters a woman's womb to be reborn, without the man actually dying (Burling, 1997, 60).

4.2.4. Metempsychosis or transmigration of souls

Metempsychosis or transmigration of souls indicates that one's life is prolonged in time by passing through different bodily existences or from another point of view; it is a life-sequence, interrupted by different reincarnations.

The *A·chiks* also believe in the transmigration of souls. The soul of a man may enter into animals like tigers, snakes, etc. If a person's soul has entered a tiger, the *Mahari* will not send information to those *chras* (maternal uncle) and relatives who are in far off places. The reason for not doing so is that they believe tigers also will come along with the *mahari* and relatives to the house of the deceased (Julius Marak, 2000, 202).

They also believe in the transmigration of souls as a state of reward and punishment. By transmigration of souls it means that when a man dies, his soul or his essence leaves the dying body and enters the body of some animal or human being as it comes into the world to begin its career. And the process may be repeated generation after generation (Milton Sangma, 1981, 227-228).

4.2.5. Reincarnation

Secondly, Reincarnation as a concept of rebirth necessarily implies the continuity of a personality. Here the human personality is regarded as continuous and accessible to memory so that when one is re-incarnated or born, one is able, at least potentially; to remember that one has lived through previous existences and these existences were one's own, that is, they had the same ego-form as the present life. As a rule, reincarnation means rebirth in a human body. Resurrection means a re-establishment of human existence after death. A new element enters here: that of change, transmutation, or transformation of one's being. Rebirth (Renovatio), the word suggests the idea of renovation, renewal, or even of improvement brought about by magical means. Rebirth may be a renewal without any change of being in its essential nature but only in its function. Another aspect is, essential transformation, which is total rebirth of the individual. Participation in the process of transformation is the fifth and the last that implicates indirect rebirth. Here the transformation is brought about not directly, by passing through death and rebirth itself, but indirectly, by participating in a process of transformation which is conceived of as taking place outside the individual (Jung, 1968, 113-14).

4.2.6. *Atchigittinga*

According to the commonly accepted doctrine of the preliterate *A·chiks* of the traditional life spirit, the conception of a happy life and death is to be reborn into the same sacred motherhood. The *A·chiks* believe in a kind of reincarnation called *Atchigittinga*. *Atchigittinga* literally means a conscious psycho-physical act of pre-planned reincarnation of the self. It is a secret *A·chik* doctrine of conscious trans-incarnation of the human *jachri* or *jabirong*. *Jabirong* literally means self-active, self-mobile, self-projecting. *Jachri* literally means self-acting, self-propelling. *Jabirong* and *jachri* mean the one and the same thing, which is the self-cognitive, self-acting human psyche or human pre-spirit (Rongmuthu, 2011, 3).

General Ellard in his book, *Christian Life and Worship* writes that "the acid test of a man's attitude towards life is his attitude towards death" (qtd. in Rongmuthu, 2011, 111).

Atchigittinga proves that one's existing body, which is like an illusion, exists only due to one's spirit and when the human spirit consciously and deliberately changes its earthly vestment, the human spirit is undying and permanent in all states. Without the human psyche of the spirit being eternal and imperishable, the psycho-physical doctrine of *Atchigittinga* is unthinkable. *Atchigittinga* evidently and conclusively proves that the human psyche or spirit naturally belonged to the millennium, when the Earth was a cloud, a breath of fresh air, an embryo in the womb of the Universe (Rongmuthu, 2011, 113).

4.2.7. *Jabirong* or *Jachri*

Conscious projection and engraftment of one's *Jabirong* or *Jachri* in the womb of a woman in any place, near or distant, can also be one's involuntary but conscious psycho-physical act. It can happen through hereditary transmission to any untrained persons, especially to any child under teens.

The person, whose life becomes psychically bifurcated through such involuntary psycho-physical phenomena inevitably becomes lean, thin, haggard-looking, weak and emancipated, and, if nothing tangible is done by person's straying, the self same person dies after due parturition. The child in whose body the person's migrated *jachri* lies, engrafted, lives on and grow into another full-fledged individual human being (Rongmuthu, 2011, 113).

In order to lure back the involuntary but consciously migrated *jachri* or *jabirong* of a person to its original niche, the preliterate *A·chiks* used to perform a solemn rite of sanctity, known as *Jaoka*, *Jaringa* or *Chidema*, which literally means 'retrieving' the straying human psyche (Rongmuthu, 2011, 114).

4.2.8. Rebirth

The *A·chiks* believe in rebirth. The souls of the dead go to a place known to them as *Mangru-Mangram-Chitmang-Bri-Balmang-Chiga* (the land of the spirits) along with the things that are given to the dead at the time of death. The souls of the dead are believed to take rest and have their midday meals on their way to the land of the spirits. This very place of resting is called *Me·mang Mesal Cha·ram-Boldak-Matchu-Karam*. It is a common occurrence amongst the *A·chiks* that the relative of the dead becomes unconscious at the time of death. Some persons, either men or woman stay unconscious for about ten to fifteen minutes. These persons testify that they accompanied the soul of the dead half the distance, as far as *Me·mang Mesal Cha·ram Boldak-Matchu-Karam* where they take their midday meals and then proceed to the land of the spirits. The *Sae-Dina-Mangga-Dine* (god of death) comes to fetch every soul before its death and takes him or her to the place of the spirits (Julius Marak, 2000, 200).

At the birth of every child a spirit is said to leave purgatory. A certain conception of punishment and reward hereafter is not wanting in their beliefs, for sin in one's life affects the form of incarnation in the next. The lowest form of re-incarnation is in the shape of insects and plants. The next higher birth is in the shape of animals and birds and then in the human form. The greatest reward for a virtuous life is to be born into the same motherhood as before (Playfair, 1998, 80).

Julius Marak states that the dead body of a person is never taken out of the house by taking out the legs first, but by the head first. This is done because of the belief in rebirth. While carrying the dead for cremation, all the streamlets that are crossed are tied across with threads. The tying of thread across the streams is intended to indicate that they have been bridged so that the spirits of the dead may go across. If a thread is tied across the stream, then the departed soul will be able to find its way to the land of the spirits. Therefore, the tying of threads across the streams and rivers is essential (Julius Marak, 2000, 204 - 205).

It is believed that the spirit of the person who commits suicide by hanging will be reincarnated in the form of a beetle, which is condemned to eat nothing but the sap or gum of the plant which provided the fibre from which the rope was made. If the death is caused by an elephant or tiger, the spirit goes to *Chitmang*, but is reincarnated in the form of the animal that caused the death (Julius Marak, 2000, 69).

Again, any person who has been killed by a tiger, elephant or by falling from a tree, or by drowning or has any other kind of unnatural death will not be taken inside the house. Some people bury or cremate such people without bringing them back to the village. Even if the corpse is brought to the village, it is laid outside the house or on the verandah. The house or the place where such a corpse is kept is called *Manggual* (Julius Marak, 2000, 202). In neither of the above cases will the spirit again inhabit a human body. The spirit of a murderer is condemned to reside in *Chitmang* for seven generations before returning to the human form (Playfair 1998, 105).

If a man has committed wrong in his life time, he may, as a punishment, be born again in the form of an animal, but this does not preclude the possibility of the spirit returning to the human shape after the death of the animal and a second sojourn at *Chitmang* (Milton Sangma, 1981, 230).

The duration of probation at *Chitmang* and the manner of the return to earth appear to depend either on the cause of the person's death, or upon the sins he committed during his life-time (Playfair, 1998, 104).

The favourite wood for burning a body is that of *the mandal* tree (Erythrina Suberosa). It is believed that if the corpse is burned with bad wood, the spirit in its reincarnation will have bad health. The burning of the body with *Simul* tree (cotton) is believed to bring bad luck to the spirit. *Boldak* tree (Schima Walichii) causes itching and irritation to the spirit; the *Agatchi* tree (Dilennis pentazyna) causes sorrow and tears for it is full of water or sap. Hard wood is preferred as it is thought that its flame is of greater help to the spirit than the soft one. In reality however, all wood is used without distinction (Julius Marak, 2000, 69).

Near the cremation place a bull is kept tethered to a post called *Gilmrong*[21] (it is also called *Kilmrong* or *Tilta)*, and when the last part of the body is about to be consumed by the fire, the animal is killed so that its spirit may accompany the spirit of the dead person and be of service to it in the next world (Milton Sangma, 1981, 250).

A dog is sacrificed to be a guide to the departed on his long journey to *Chitmang*. If the dead be of some one great, especially a woman, bullocks must be offered at the moment of the lighting of the pyre, one on the spot, and others by signal at surrounding hamlets (Carey, 1993, 25).

Robbins Burling is also of the opinion that side by side with this concept of an after-world is the belief that the soul can somehow be born again into this world, and even into the same family. Occasionally, people recognize a sign such as a birth mark, which shows them that a baby has been reborn from an earlier existence, since someone also, may have had similar marks. A soul occasionally deserts a man's body and enters a woman's womb to be reborn, without the man first actually being dead. During this process the man grows thin and weak and if nothing is done, he or she will die when the baby is born. The belief in the transference of the soul from one person to another also figures in the custom, when a man or a woman dies, of presenting a gift to the house where he or she was raised (Julius Marak, 2000, 68).

It is an age-old belief of the *A·chiks* that the spirit of a dead alone is not warmly welcomed by the spirits of the relatives and friends of the deceased who had gone there

---

[21] A 'Y' shaped post planted upright near the place of cremation where a bull is kept tethered before it is being killed; a sacrificial post.

before, in the holy and happy regions of the *Dal·gipa Nalsa* (Great Beyond), if the disembodied spirit of the deceased is not accompanied by the spirit of the cow. Therefore, cows which are fit to accompany the spirits of human beings into the holy and happy spheres of the Great Beyond are sacred to the *A·chiks*. With such a belief, the *A·chiks* kill cows at funerals and at the *Mangona*. This practice of cow-killing at funerals and at post-funeral ceremonies is followed by the *A·chiks*, only to release the bovine spirit so that it may accompany the spirit of the deceased to the spirit sphere (Rongmuthu, 1996, 6).

The belief of the *A·chiks* in life after death is so strong that till today, the *A·chiks* throw or give food and other materials of daily use to the spirits of the dead to carry them along to *Balpakram* or *Napak*, the final resting place of the spirits. The *A·chiks* believe that the body dies but the spirit remains forever and one will be reborn again as human beings or in some other form (Julius Marak, 2000, 104).

If the funeral rites are not performed the spirit does not go to *Chitmang*, the abode of spirits, instead it wends away on earth and turns into an evil spirit and reincarnation is a remote possibility. Even in the next life it is made a slave of other spirits and if reincarnated at all, it is born to be poor and has to live a hard life on earth. It is also believed that the spirit loses its way to the *Chitmang* and therefore loses its opportunity and the way to return to the same clan, family or relative in the next incarnation (Paulinus Marak, 2005, 104).

In the beginning men and women remained immortal. It was *Me·gam Gairipa Mande Singeripa Me·gam Dimrang Chada Gongman Mande Dimrim Me·gam Dimsim* who first tasted death among human beings. One day *Megam Gairipa* went to the market at *Dimrimpatal Chalangagal* taking with him his daughter *Gairi Singeri*. On the way *Me·gam Gairipa* captured *Rime-Rinok* (the patriarchial head of the land-lizards or iguanas) and took him as a prisoner. At midnight *Me·gam Gairipa* suddenly fell fatally ill and died. The God, *Misi Saljong,* had scourged him for capturing his servant, *Rime-Rinok*. This was the first death among mankind since the world began. *Gairi Singeri*, daughter of the deceased man, rent the air with her hysterical cries over the death of her father. She stamped the earth frantically, in great despair. In the meantime the captive made a good escape. Nobody dared to capture him again. The body of *Me·gam Gairipa* was taken to his village and cremated on a funeral pyre infront of the courtyard of his house by his fellow-villagers. After cremation, his spirit, having assumed a new appearance as fresh as a newly matured gourd of a newly-kilned earthen pot, came back home bringing back the cow and necklaces which had been given him at his death. At that time *Grimchi Bachari*, walking along with the matrilineal nephew of her husband, was scouring a stream nearby with her *chekke* (triangular fishing basket) in search of prawns. The nephew of the deceased was carrying a fish-creel for her. Meanwhile, at home, her children were sitting disconsolately on a raised side porch of the house. When they saw the apparition of their father coming towards them, they skipped about with joy and cried out to their mother that their father has come home. The mother shouted back at them saying that their father is already dead and gone, how could he ever come back?

So saying she solemnly returned to her task of collecting prawns. The spirit felt ashamed of the unmaidenly conduct of his wife in associating with his matrilineal nephew alone. So in anger, he started for *Mangru Mangram Chitmang A·song Balmang Chiga*, the temporary residence of departed spirits.

When *Grimchi Bachari* returned home, she saw the cow and the necklaces which had been brought and placed there by the spirit. She was now fully convinced of the actual return of her spouse; so she decided to pursue him. She took the route which the spirit of her husband travelled to the spirit land. She trudged onward through difficult paths. The woman sped up a mountain to the resting place of the *Ghost Bhegia* and the breathing place of *Katchi Chanapa.* The wife continued her pursuit to the clearing of *Bonepa Janepa.* Undismayed and undeterred, *Grimchi Bachari* persistently dragged on her pursuit until she came to the limbo of *Mangru Mangram.* There she overtook her husband and prayed him to return home with her. But *Me·gam Gairipa* declined, saying:

> You did not welcome me as your husband and your beloved when I last came home. I endorse your choice of my own matrilineal nephew to remarry after me. Let him marry you rightly, and let him preserve all my earthly belongings and heirlooms and faithfully perform every domestic function as a householder and as your second husband in my place. Let him complete my unfinished tasks. If you and my matrilineal relations perform all the needful funeral and post funeral rites over me and set up memorial posts for me, I will be reborn into the same motherhood, which is dearer and greater than anything else I had while I was in the land of the living (Rongmuthu, 2008, 251).

Grimchi Bachari wept bitterly for a long time at the thought of having to return home alone, meanwhile she gazed steadfastly at the receding form of her beloved husband's immortal spirit. Finally she returned home.

The belief that the soul can somehow be reborn again into this world is seen in the life of a man named *Rakda* in a village who had a son named *Dengja*. A draught caused a great famine in their village, so one day, both father and son went to a distant place, taking a couple of baskets with them, in order to do manual labour so as to be able to buy rice. The two worked hard the whole day under the scorching heat of the sun, in the field of a rich man and managed to fill their baskets with paddy in return for their earnest labours.

On their way back, father and son took a short rest under the cool shade of a peepul tree. *Dengja,* feeling very thirsty, went in search of water to drink and asked his father to wait for him. While he was away, *Rakda* wished to have more paddies in his basket and thus he took three helpings with both hands from his son's basket. Then he smoothed the paddy so that no trace of theft was noticeable. When *Dengja* returned, he was totally ignorant of what his father had done. So they continued their journey and reached their native village.

Some months later, *Rakda* fell seriously ill and died. As a conscientious and obedient son, *Dengja* performed the necessary funeral rites and set up a *Kima* (memorial post) in front of his father's house.

In the sight of the Mother Goddess *Dingipa Babra*, nothing is lost, nothing is overlooked or forgotten, but every action, thought and feeling is taken into account and recorded in a way not discernible to mortal eyes. So, in his rebirth *Rakda*, because of the theft he had committed in the land of the living, was reborn as a cow. The self same cow was made to plough his son's paddy fields. For five years the cow laboured hard and eventually died. *Dengja*, who had a vegetable garden near his house, put up the skull of the cow to be used as a scare crow.

Once in the evening a woman from *Dengja's* village entered his garden to steal some vegetables. Strangely enough the skull of the cow began to address her in the following words:

> Beware, O woman, do not steal. As a man I was *Rakda*, the father of *Dengja*. I once stole some paddy from my son's basket during the last famine. For that foul deed *Dingipa Babra* made me reborn as a cow to plough the fields of my son for full five years. As a cow I am dead now; but the debt incurred through my commission of theft is not yet fully repaid. I am still compelled to watch my son's garden like this (Rongmuthu, 2008, 88).

The woman ran off to *Dengja* almost frightened out of her wits, and told him how the skull had spoken to her. *Dengja* had a troubled mind. He went to his vegetable garden, took the skull and burned it ritually (forgave his father). Next night in a dream he heard his father asking him if he had really forgiven him. *Dengja* assured his father that he had done so. "Then let me depart in peace," answered *Rakda*. After his dream *Dengja* felt at ease. He felt that the spirit of his father had already passed completely beyond the chains and limitations of mortal life into the blissful spirit land, there to remain for a time until it is commanded by the higher spirits to be reborn as a human being into this world.

4.3. Spirit

The phenomenology of the spirit involves the third category of Jungian archetype. The word 'spirit' possesses such a wide range of applications that it requires considerable effort to make a comprehensive understanding of the various meanings it denotes. A very widespread view conceives the Spirit as a higher and psyche as a lower principle of activity. Wundt takes spirit as "the inner being, regardless of any connection with an outer being." It also means "the sum-total of all the phenomena of rational thought, or of the intellect, including the will, memory, imagination, creative power, and aspirations motivated by ideals" (Jung, 1968, 208). Spirit has the further connotation of sprightliness, as when we say that a person is 'spirited', meaning that he is versatile and full of ideas, with a brilliant, witty, and surprising turn of mind.

William Carey in *The Garo Jungle Book* (1993, 2nd ed.) states that spirits form a major body of myths and archetypes in *A·chik* narratives. They believed in a multitude of benevolent and malevolent spirits. Each spirit is known by several names. The spirits are collectively referred to as *mite* which are everywhere such as above the sky, on the earth beneath, in the depths of the waters, in the dark caverns, in the recesses of mysterious mountains and hills, trees and bamboo groves, rivers and lakes, shrubs, sticks and stones, all these are the dwelling places of some spirits. Similarly, the stars, the sun and the moon are associated with some spirits or *mites* and all these *mites* are considered as immortal beings by the *A·chiks* (Thomas, 1995, 203). The destiny of man, from birth to death, is governed by a host of such spirits who must be duly propitiated, by sacrifices of varied nature and at various occasions of their life time (Milton

Sangma, 1981, 220). They attach much importance to the worship of the spirits which rule the seasons, to maintain harmony with the spirits and thus obtain their blessings in the form of good harvests. Certain mountains are feared as the special abode of departed spirits. Deep waters are similarly regarded with superstitious dread because of the demon which is believed to be at the bottom in a golden boat. The number of *mites* are gradually increasing just as the number of septs or sub clans are increasing amongst the *A·chiks*. The same *mite* may be known by different names in different clans. There are as many as 230 names of *mites* from the different clans (Sinha, 1966, 48).

Some names of *mites* or spirits are as follows: *A·tila mite, Susime mite, Chura mite, Jang·kepang mite, Sildam mite, Salbamon mite, Udim mite, Joga A·ding mite, Bang mite, A·rata mite, Risi mite, Rangsan mite, Sangprong or Galapa nagande mite, A·song mite, Kram mite, Rongdik mite, Wa·ge mite, Darechik mite, Bangkni mite, Skal mite, Goera wa·kep mite, Chual mite, Saljong mite, Tongrengma mite, Ro·ong mite, A·ni mati mite, Brara mite, Lengra Basali mite, Rakwa mite, Chendi Chakinga mite, Bilwatok mite, Do·chi gitok mite, Rama E·sumu mite, Choro Chong·kampek mite, Songading mite, A·se mite, Bidawe mite, Jaropak mite, Skaldu mite, Pakmasam mite, Ganna mite, Kram mite*, etc (Mihir Sangma, 1994, 54).

Several peaks are the abodes of deities. In *A·chik* pantheon diverse spirits exist, such as the gods of wind and storm, gods of rain, serpent spirits in great rivers, rock and cave spirits, water nymphs and fairies, fiends and ghosts and other images of nature. Sacred places and groves, haunted by the spirits, are marked. Some spirits are considered to be the originators of cultivation and woodcraft, musical arts and dance, medical and medicinal formulae and war and peace. Such techniques and arts were learned from their gods by their forefathers. Headhunting, renowned in the past, was a religious institution connected with fertility rites. Other deities of hunting, fertility, wealth and wisdom receive appropriate offerings (Joshi, 2004, 150).

Their knowledge and technological skills enable the *A·chiks* to draw sustenance from the natural environment in which they live. They are also surrounded by a spiritual environment. Though the *A·chiks* are remarkably uncertain of the nature of spirits, they know that they must behave in appropriate ways if the disaster is not to overtake them. Other than *me·mang* (ghost), the *A·chiks* have only one general term *mite* for supernatural beings; but this covers both beings whom we would call gods and certain lesser, quite different nuisances, which hardly deserve to be known by any term more dignified than spirit. The latter, distinguished from the gods as 'the *mite* that bites', are numerous and ubiquitous, and when they bite, they cause disease (Burling, 1997, 54).

They have an idea of a supernatural world that consists of the deities and spirits (*mite*) and the spirit of the dead - *me·mang. Mite*, when pleased, showers blessings and benefits on people, whereas when they are displeased or enraged, they cause illness, failure of crops, and damage to houses or village by storms, lightning or other natural calamities. When the 'spirit bites', the *A·chiks* say *mite chika*, which is a symptom of diseases or calamities indicating the spirit that causes them and the kind of actions or sacrifices to be performed for propitiating the concerned *mite* (Paulinus Marak, 2005, 70). The *A·chiks* must behave appropriately to pre-empt any disaster by the enraged *mite*.

The *A·chiks* maintain that innumerable deities (*mite*) inhabit the earth. The deities are normally invisible. Occasionally they appear in people's dreams and at times even in real life. *Dakkara*, the deity of creation, manifests himself as a man with a long beard. *Risi*, the deity who is associated with a particular *kram* (a kind of drum) can show up as a woman. Other deities appear as animals. Some of these animals are vicious (tigers, electric eels, monster lizards), others benign (goats, peacocks). There are also deities that relate to plants. An example is the deity *Goera*, who is associated with the sleep inducing *dikge* (medicinal herb). Again other deities manifest themselves in phenomena such as lightning and thunder, earthquakes, gales or the raging fire that burns the newly cleared swiddens (Paulinus Marak, 2005, 47).

The vast majority of deities are not known by name. They are referred to in relation to the object that such a deity is believed to be associated with, for example, the deity of the rice storage vessel *Rong·dikni mite* or the place that a deity is thought to reside in the house *nokni mite*, the deities of the jungle *burungni mite* (Paulinus Marak, 2005, 48).

As Burling mentions, these *mites* live in many places. Some dwell in villages, others in the jungle, near a tree, or by the stream or a waterfall. A fork in a road is a favourite place for the deities. The powerful *mites* are said to live on mountain tops. All deities are dealt with same general fashion, though the details of the sacrifices differ. Several men usually spend two hours building an altar. Most altars are built of bamboo and leaves, but the precise form depends upon the particular spirit to whom the sacrifice is directed (1997, 55-56).

Not all the supernatural beings are as uniformly malignant as the biting *mite*. Most of the others, the 'creating' *mites* as they are occasionally called, are more or less neutral if not positively friendly. They are a bit more remote from daily life, but harmony between men and these gods, as they are appropriately called, must be maintained by several annual sacrifices (Burling, 1997, 58).

Milton Sangma mentions how the *A·chiks* fear the occurrence of natural phenomena like thunder, lightning, earthquake, eclipse, wind, rain and shooting stars. They believe that each of these natural forces is controlled by a spirit. These natural phenomena are not, in themselves, the objects of their worship or sacrifice, but since each of these events is controlled by a spirit, sacrifices must be offered to these spirits and their favour gained. Thus sacrifices are offered to the rain-god when rain is required and to sun-god when sunshine is needed.

The *A·chiks* are very religious and god-fearing people. They believe that all physical ailments, accidents and unnatural deaths are due to the wrath of one or the other malevolent spirit. Therefore, sacrifices of animals and birds must be offered to the deities to appease them as well as to invoke their blessings (Milton Sangma, 1981, 233).

4.3.1. *Tatara Rabuga Stura Pantura*

The *A·chiks* believe in the existence of a Supreme Deity who is sometimes identified as *Tatara Rabuga*. He is the greatest of all the deities and spirits of the *A·chik* pantheon. *Dakgipa Rugipa Stugipa Pantugipa* is the Supreme Creator. The *A·chiks* believe in creation of heaven and the earth and all living beings. According to stages of creation of different objects which was completed within eight days, the Creator was named by eight different names. On the first day *A·gilbo chigilboko dakchengo* (Creation of the Universe), God was known as *Tatara Rabuga Stura Pantura* or *Dakgipa Rugipa Stugipa Pantugipa*. The second day, *A·ko bisil kao, chiko waring dako* (separated the land from water); God was called *Nostu*

Nopantu Misi Siste. On the third day, *A·ni prem chini jimjemko* (Creation of all living beings on earth and the ocean, except man), God was known as *Norebak Norekdim* and *Jipjini Japjana*. On the fourth day God was called as *Aijangga Reding Banda* or *Norimjak Nosiksak* for He created *Sal, ja* and *askirangko* (Creation of all heavenly bodies). God was known as *Asima Dingsima Drama Chisama Dempema Demjima* on the fifth day for He created *Sam-bol* (Creation of plants and vegetation). On the sixth day God created *Mande* (man) so He was known as *Ba·bra* or *Rabuga Ranaga*. On the seventh day God created the lesser god and goddess of wealth, food crops: *Patigipa Ra·rongipa Ruragipa Kontogipa miterangko* - so He was known as *Susimema Sangkildoma*. God was known as *Rekroni Rekrona* on the eighth day for he created the supernatural powers of dread, fear and misfortunes: *Bon·atgipa Chon·atgipa skalrang*. The Creator, *Dakgipa Rugipa Stugipa Pantugipa* ended the work which He had done, and rested on the ninth day from all His works and blessed and sanctified it in the form of a festival, known as *Drua Wanbola* or *Wangala* (Mihir Sangma, 1994, 48 -49).

Tatara-Rabuga is the creator at whose command the world was made by two lesser spirits, *Nostu-Nopantu* and *Machi* (Thomas, 1995, 203). He is looked upon as the greatest of the spirits, and his own special mission with regard to the welfare of man, is the curing of wasting diseases such as *Kala-azar* and other persistent fevers. He is known by eight other names, namely *Stura-Pantura, Jipjini-Jipjana, Kuradok-Kurapin, Chandasi-Gongongrigipa, Bulgipa-Imbanggipa, Ajanjan-Buljanjan, Sekira-Balira* and *Jamanokgipa-Janginibiambi* (Playfair, 1998, 81). The *A·chiks* call him by about one hundred and sixty names in total, of which the following are some: *Tatara-Rabuga, Bisikrom Bidatare, Rabugama, Ranagama, Stura Pantura, A·ning Randinima, Ambi Mori, Dakdame, Rurime,*

Dakgipa Rugipa, Aiti, Biati, Korabok Kosapin, Maresu Marebok, Dingipa, Babra, Ba·rangipa, Chitragipa, Nirikgipa, Sandigipa, Ja·rikgipa, Ja·sangipa, Janggini Nokgipa, Jamani Biambi, Pattigipa, Ra·rongipa, Sualgipa, Imbagipa, Mikbegipa, Mitdakgipa, Ja·ragipa, Ja·chitgipa, Rakkigipa Nirokgipa, Chichrigipa Rakkigipa, Chijanggiko Ripinggipa, Chichrigipa Rakkigipa, Chijanggiko Kangipa, Chichriko On·gipa, Jikmite Gosai, Ma·gipa Jagring (Paulinus Marak, 2005, 28-29).

Rabuga, Ranaga, Tatara or *Dakgipa* are used as names for the god who is believed to have made the world and man. *Dakgipa*, in fact, means quite literally 'the one who makes' (Burling, 1997, 58). There is a multiple number of beneficent and malevolent *mite*. The anger of any *mite* must be appeased by offering a sacrifice (Julius Marak, 2000, 53). An expensive sacrifice is offered to him by killing a bull, goat and a fowl. Rice beer and rice are also provided for the people during the ceremony which lasts for two days (Milton Sangma, 2002-2003, V. Pg 1).

Besides *Tatara-Rabuga*, there are other principal deities and spirits who are of great significance to the religious minded *A·chiks*.

4.3.2. *Saljong*

Saljong was supreme among the gods under whom there were other gods and goddesses entrusted with specific functions. The heavenly bodies like the Sun, the Moon and the Stars were believed to preside over the hills and were considered as the agents of *Saljong* to manage the affairs of the world (Bhattacharjee, 1978, 5). He is the giver of all materials to human beings and all other living beings on earth, in the water and above the earth (Paulinus Marak, 2005, 29). He is represented by the sun. He is responsible for the germination and growth of all crops, trees and bamboo and for the ripening of all fruits and grains. He is the Lord of the harvest, and the greatest *A·chik* festival, *Wangala,* is celebrated in his honour after the harvest (Thomas, 1995, 204). The actual sacrifice is offered to him in the fields before the village festival begins. On the sacrificial altar, liquor is poured out on the ground infront of it and the worshippers then return to the village for the festival rejoicing (Rana, 1989, 217). The spirit is also known by the names *Tengsugipa-Tengtotgipa, Salgira, Salgra* and *Rengra-Balsa* (Playfair, 1998, 81). *Saljong* controls the water and the rain and the growth of all things. When the dried fields are burned before planting, *Saljong* sees the smoke of the fire and comes to join the people as they worship him in their fields. *Saljong* is not an ordinary biting spirit. The blindness which he causes is incurable. He is no less powerful than *Rabuga* (Burling 1997, 58).

4.3.3. *Nostu-Nopantu*

Nostu-Nopantu is the deity, who at the command of *Tatara-Rabuga*, fashioned the earth with the help of another spirit, named *Machi* (Playfair, 1998, 81). But no sacrifice is offered to them as they do not harm any man (Milton Sangma, 2002-2003, Vol. V. 1).

4.3.4. *Chorabudi*

Chorabudi is a benign spirit and is the protector of crops. He is invoked against pains in the ears and boils. He is the servant of *Tatara-Rabuga* (Thomas, 1995, 204). Before partaking of the first fruits of the season, such as Indian corn, millet and melons, a small quantity of some of these is always presented as an offering to him. Sacrifices are offered to him for curing the diseases of the ears, and of boils (Milton Sangma, 2002-2003, Vol. V. 1).

4.3.5. *Goera*

Goera is the spirit of strength and the cause of thunder and lightning. He is prayed to, for health and strength after long illness (Playfair, 1998, 81). He destroys human beings, trees and animals by causing lightning in the open fields. Sacrifices are offered to him with pig, fowl or duck which is offered to him at the foot of a tree. According to the belief of the *A·chiks*, lightning and thunder is caused by the spirit of *Goera*. Lightning is caused by the flashing of *Goera*'s sword. *Goera* formerly lived on earth and slew a monster pig as big as a mountain. Afterwards however he ascended to the skies and amuses himself from time to time in martial exercises with the sword. Thunder is the noise he makes while taking exercise with his sword (Milton Sangma, 1981, 235).

4.3.6. *Kalkame*

Kalkame is the elder brother of *Goera* and is entrusted with the care of the lives of all men on earth. He guarantees safety from dangers from wild animals, aquatic animals and all kinds of dangers and diseases. The *A·song* or the sacrificial stones are erected in his honour (Thomas, 1995, 204). They pray to him in the *A·songtata* or *A·songroka* ceremony, and is entreated to keep the people of the village safe from all dangers of the forest during the coming year.

The offering is made on sacrificial stones which are smeared with the blood of the victim (Playfair, 1998, 82). This deity is entrusted with certain power that enables it to cause some misfortunes upon a person in order to draw him closer towards him. However, if this fails, death is the only penalty for that person. This same God is also locally known as *Gana mite* or simply *Gana* for whom they perform the sacrificial offering and prayer with certain rites, rituals and divine services. This ceremony is locally known as *Gana* ceremony which is the only means of saving one from misfortune or death penalty (Mihir Sangma 2004, 166).

4.3.7. *Susime*

Susime, a female deity, is the giver of both good and bad things to mankind. She is believed to cause and cure blindness, lameness, deafness and other diseases. She is represented by the moon (Thomas, 1995, 204). *Susime mite* causes chills and fever alternately. To drive it away, an altar of bamboo and leaves must be built in the yard infront of the house. A pig or chicken is sacrificed at this altar and the animal is cooked and eaten after the ceremony. When a spirit, known as '*but*', causes an attack of dysentery, a small boat is built of bamboo, dabbed with the blood of a sacrificial animal, and floated down the river; and the spirit is supposed to follow it. Other *mites* are held responsible for paleness, lassitude, skin diseases and all the other aches and pains which plague the *A·chiks*. Each can be pacified with a special form of sacrifice. *Susime* is associated with the moon, and, may blind people or lame them, but the disease caused by this god can be cured by sacrifice (Burling, 1997, 59). She is also an expert in instigating people to quarrel and fight among themselves (Milton Sangma 2002-2003, Vol.V.1).

4.3.8. *Asima-Dingsima*

Asima-Dingsima is the mother of *Susime*. She does not possess any power and no sacrifice is, therefore, offered to her (Thomas, 1995, 204). The other names for this spirit are *Norekbak-Norekdim, Sonakale-Kaburanche and Mikrongitok-Kisangsitok* (Playfair, 1998, 82). It is believed that it is inauspicious to pronounce her name and also that it is taboo. However, she is regarded as a famous goddess, as the constellation of heaven and stars had attended her funeral ceremony which lasted for many days (Milton Sangma, 2002-2003, Vol.V.1- 2).

4.3.9. *Tongrengma*

Tongrengma, a female deity, has the power to cause ailment to human lives. When she causes ailment, a sphincter is formed and the sick patient suffers from unbearable pain. A cock is offered to appease her near a river or a stream (Milton Sangma, 2002-2003, Vol.V.2).

4.3.10. *Nawang*

Nawang is an evil spirit who devours the souls of human beings on the way to the purgatory just after death. When a person dies it is customary for the *A·chiks* to throw ornaments and money along with the deceased, so that the deceased man can proceed easily to purgatory, while the *Nawang* spirit is busy collecting those materials. This evil spirit roams about the earth trying to devour souls whenever any soul comes across him. Sometimes he is in human form and sometimes he comes in the form of

Maldengong (a mythical animal). He also causes stomach pain, vomiting, diarrhoea and is believed to be at a man's death bed, ready to devour him when he dies (Playfair, 1998, 82).

4.3.11. *Salgira*

Salgira is associated with the sun and is less troublesome than his brother *Susime*, and so he receives no sacrifices (Burling, 1997, 59).

4.3.12. *Dingipa Babra Mugipa Jaring*

The *A·chiks* believe that the destiny of every human being has been preordained by the Divine Mother *Dingipa Babra Mugipa Jaring*, and the great mathematical thinker, who has also fashioned the size, height, looks and constitution of each living person. At the birth of every child, the spirits of the elemental world and the spirits of all living beings muster under *Dingipa Babra*. They spread out their mysteriously woven webs to ascertain whose lot it shall be to cut off the life of the new born babe. This mysteriously woven web is known as *Rechu* or *Amrechu* (plantain leaf) that is, the Web of Destiny. At the birth of every human being a spirit called *Kalkame Kalgra* takes charge of the child. It is he who protects the child throughout its life. At the time of death, *Kalkame Kalgra* gives away the person to whosoever's lot it is to cut off the life of the child concerned (Rongmuthu, 2008, 115).

4.4. Trickster

The trickster is an object of study in mythology, religion, anthropology, psychology, and recently in film as well. The trickster is a divinity or semi-divine creature that pops up in almost every mythology or folklore of the world. It is the god of the crossroads, or of trade, of mischief, the physical representation of randomness, and an agent of chaos. At the same time, as being short-sighted, impulse-driven, and an instigator of disorder, he often plays tricks on other gods or nature. He is also a bringer of knowledge, steals fire from the gods, and is someone who, by breaking the rules, creates new ones. Paul Radin explains that the trickster is at one and the same time a creator and destroyer, giver and negator, he who dupes others and who is always himself duped (Flam, 2011, 4).

Jung studied the trickster as a basic human archetype. He believed that it was part of a collective unconscious shared by the human race. He surmised that the trickster represented our own basic nature, the animal in us that we had left behind, as we learned to master tools and fire. In psychology the trickster has been referred to as a sort of id, a shadow of our true nature (Flam, 2011, 5).

The myth of the trickster is the story of a man trapped by, and incapable of dealing with the circumstances of his surroundings. During his travels he meets tricksters who tricked him, because he lacks the necessary knowledge to see through their deceptions, until he has learned sufficiently to turn the con on his assailants, cause upheaval in the normal order of things, and be recognized as the legendary fool. The development of the trickster through the narrative is the story of an animal that is driven by his impulses, troubled by them, learns from them and can use them in dealing with the world, rather than being used by them and having the world to deal with him (Flam, 2011, 13).

The Trickster-Figure, which is the fourth category of archetype in Jung's analysis, is a clown, a mischief maker. He provides the comic relief that a story often needs to offset heavy dramatic tension. The trickster can be an ally or companion of the hero, or may work for the villain. In some instances the trickster may even be the hero or villain. In any role, the trickster usually represents the cunning forces, and is pitied against the opponents who are stronger or more powerful. According to Jung:

> The typical trickster motifs are his fondness for sly jokes and malicious pranks, his power as a shape-shifter, his dual nature, half-animal, half divine, his exposure to all kinds of torture, and last but not the least - his approximation of the figure of a saviour (Jung, 1968, 264).

The trickster is a primordial 'cosmic' being of divine-animal nature, on the one hand superior to man because of his superhuman qualities, and, on the other, inferior to him because of his irrational and unconscentiousness.

In *A·chik* folk narrative, one finds a human and animal trickster who deceives others for his own benefit. For instance, Simison Sangma speaks of *Gangbo Nokma* (a rich man named *Gangbo*) who deceives his neighbours through sly ways and becomes rich, while the neighbours get tricked and lose everything they have (Simison Sangma, 1984, 14). There are also instances of animal tricksters such as the *Mikkol* (monkey) trying to entice young girls *Nose* and *Dimse* (Dhoronsing Sangma, 1988, 32). And it also deceives people as well as animals like *Matchadu* (tigerman) (Dhoronsing Sangma, 1988, 35).

Dewangsing Rongmuthu in *The Epiclore of the Garos* (2008) narrates various episodes to illustrate the different activities of the tricksters through different stories. Stories are an important aspect of culture. Many works of art and most works of literature tell stories. Stories are of ancient origin, existing in ancient Egypt, ancient Greece, Chinese, and Indian cultures. Stories are also a ubiquitous component of human communication, used as parables and examples used to illustrate points. Story telling was probably one of the earliest forms of entertainment.

4.4.1. *Gangbo Nokma*[22]

Gangbo nokma was very wealthy and powerful; he was a quick-witted, crafty, pragmatic and proud individual. Because of his haughty domineering ways, he was extremely unpopular with his neighbours. Though outwardly they feared him, inwardly they wished his ruin. One day all the elders of the village held a secret meeting in which a plan was hatched to burn *Gangbo Nokma's* house with himself and his whole family in it. The imminent victim of this sinister design got scent of it and secretly removed all his money, jewels and riches and buried them in a nearby forest. All valuable articles were quietly removed to convenient places. And the man went about as if he was wholly ignorant of the intrigue against him.

The next night the enemies of *Gangbo Nokma* fastened the doors of his house from outside and set it on fire. However, *Gangbo* and his family escaped unscathed through an opening in the back wall which he had previously

---

[22] A rich man named *Gangbo*, who deceives his neighbours through sly ways and becomes rich.

prepared. The next morning he assumed the role of a completely ruined man. He told the villagers that the ashes of his house were all that he could call his own. He filled up a dozen or more sacks with the ashes of his house and carried them in the direction of the market. The villagers had seen him carry away the ashes; but they were not interested in what he would do with them. *Gangbo* himself dug up all his money and precious jewels and proudly marched into the village with them in broad daylight. He began to count all his coins and proudly displayed his jewels in the sight of all the villagers. The villagers were surprised at his sudden acquisition of wealth and they eagerly asked him how he came by it. He replied:

> The ashes of our dwellings are in great demand by some foreign merchants in the market town. It was very fortunate that my house was burnt. Its ashes brought me more money than I ever had before. You should remember that what seem apparently to be calamities are often blessings in disguise (Rongmuthu, 2008, 12).

Gangbo argued with the villagers in such a convincing manner that they at once burnt up their own dwellings with all they had in them and filled the sacks with the ashes. Then they marched together to the market and offered the ashes for sale. The market people laughed derisively at the villagers and looked upon them as lunatics for wanting to sell such useless things as ashes. At this the villagers were enraged at *Gangbo.* They returned home empty handed and were determined to kill *Gangbo's* cattle and eat them up. *Gangbo* himself met the villagers and politely expressed sorrow that the foreign merchants who dealt in ashes had departed from the locality, and asked the villagers not to think of him as someone who thought of doing wrong to them and said "Pray do not think of doing any wrong to me or else something may happen to you in the long run" (Rongmuthu, 2008, 12).

The villagers would not listen to his entreaty, but forcibly took away all his cattle and slaughtered them. *Gangbo* implored them to be merciful enough to spare him the skins of the slain animals. They granted his request, since they had no use for the skins. *Gangbo* took the skins of his slain cattle, dried them in the sun, punctured some of them so that they might appear more useless than ever, made strong bags out of the remaining ones and marched out of the village. *Gangbo* came upon a rich cultivator who was ploughing his field. *Gangbo* introduced himself as a travelling leather merchant who was ready to buy good and bad skins alike, and asked the man for a drink of water. The farmer directed him to his house saying that his children were there and would give him a drink. *Gangbo* went to the farmer's house and told the man's children that their father had sent him for his money and jewels. The children refused to show the stranger the place where his father's wealth was stored. *Gangbo* then yelled out to the farmer saying: "They say they will not give it." The farmer, busy as he was with his ploughing, did not bother about what his children were really refusing to give the stranger. He simply surmised that they were denying the man a mere drink of water. So he brandished the stick with which he had been goading the animals and cried out angrily at the children, "If you don't give it to him, I'll use this stick on you!" (Rongmuthu, 2008, 13)

The children obediently showed *Gangbo* a big earthen pitcher filled to the brim with money, but sealed at the mouth. *Gangbo* speedily broke the seal, poured out all the shining coins into his crude bags, rolled these inside the pieces of punctured hides and marched off towards the cultivator to allay the suspicion of the children. He thanked the man for the drink of water which in reality he had not taken, and joyfully made his way back home to his native village, now a richer man than ever.

Gangbo eventually reached his village, poured out all his coins from the leather bag in the presence of the villagers and began to count before their eyes. The onlookers were amazed at the immense money he exhibited and asked him how he acquired such a huge fortune. He replied that if they wanted to become rich, they should kill their cattle, skin the slain beasts, puncture the skins, go and sell them in the market.

The credulous villagers straight away killed all their cattle, dried their skins, bored them through and through and took them to the market but nobody there wanted to buy the skins. The villagers were taken to be crazy fools for attempting to sell such useless punctured skins.

While the villagers were at the market, *Gangbo* set out towards the same place, to enjoy their embarrassment. On the outskirts of the market he met a travelling cloth merchant who sold rare and precious cloth on credit, if he felt satisfied with the house of the purchaser. Now, near the wayside was a cluster of well-built houses, whose owners were all in the market. *Gangbo* entered one of these houses and asked some small children for a drink of water. He seated himself on the porch while the children fetched water. As he drank *Gangbo* talked freely with the children as if they were his own. The cloth seller approached *Gangbo* for making a sale. *Gangbo* said that he was really in need of cloth, but at that moment he had no cash to make the purchase. Thereupon the merchant graciously offered to let him have some valuable cloth on credit. He asked *Gangbo* to show him his house and to give his name as well as the name of his father. So *Gangbo* politely showed the house where he happened to be and said that his name was *On·jawa* (will not give) and that his father's name was *Man·jawa* (will not get). The merchant took the names and said that he would return in a year for payment. After twelve months, the merchant did return to the place for the payment of the house owner, when the latter not only denied all knowledge of *On·jawa* and *Man·jawa*, but became angry with the insistent merchant, belaboured with the help of the neighbours and left him half-dead (Rongmuthu, 2008, 14-15).

Gangbo dressed himself in the rarest clothes and appeared like a man about to be married. In the meantime, his co-villagers, who had been ridiculed at the market place for attempting to sell punctured cattle skins, were returning to the village with unbridled wrath. On the way they solemnly vowed that they would straight away put the deceitful man to death in the cruelest possible way. They decided to bind him up and put in a bamboo basket and drown him in a pond far away from their village.

When the angry villagers arrived home, they saw *Gangbo* attired in his new clothes. Wasting no words, they seized him, tied him up and thrust him into the basket and carried it away to a distant pond. When they reached the spot, they were very tired and hungry, and so they decided to eat. They put down the basket on the bank and walked a few yards away to take their meal. As soon as the villagers were out of sight a young cowherd came along and curiously examined the strange basket and found *Gangbo* inside and asked him what he was doing. The artful captive replied in a mournful voice that he was being taken by force under the orders of the king to be the bridegroom of a beautiful princess. The boy listened with open mouth. *Gangbo* added that he was in love with a poor peasant girl and he did not think of encumbering himself with power and riches by marrying king's daughter. This cowherd had been leading a very hard life, minding a large number of cows and calves every day. He was amazed at the wonderful things *Gangbo* revealed to him and thought that the man was a fool to decline marrying a princess merely for sentimental reasons. So the boy said "were I in your place, I would fly like a bird to the palace even now. Why not send me as a substitute?" (Rongmuthu, 2008, 16)

Gangbo expressed willingness and asked the boy to untie him and the boy exchanged his tattered clothes for the gorgeous wedding apparel, put him in the basket and asked the boy to remain silent if they asked him any question. *Gangbo* went away with the cattle towards his village. After finishing their repast the villagers returned to the spot where they had left the basket. Without examining the basket they kicked the basket into the pond, watched the bubbles rising in the spot where it went down, and danced with savage joy at the thought that at last they had got rid of their intrepid foe.

The wonderment of the villagers knew no bounds, however, when, on reaching home, they discovered *Gangbo* in possession of fine cows, bulls and calves. They were stupefied at the sight and could not utter a word. *Gangbo*, perceiving their thoughts said:

> I thank you heartily for putting me in possession of this herd. Under the charmed pond, there lies a wonderful village where there are such fine cows, bullocks and calves a galore. Their owners are all anxious to exchange them for bamboo-threads which they highly prized. If any one of you dare

> go down deep into the pool, securely bound in the
> bamboo-baskets so that no aquatic animal may harm
> you on the way, you will certainly obtain a similar
> herd of cattle (Rongmuthu, 2008, 17).

The villagers' nodded assent and commenced to make big bamboo baskets for themselves. With their own hands they carried the completed baskets to the spot where they had kicked *Gangbo* into the water. They brought a lot of food and rice-beer and made merry in anticipation of the huge herd of cows which would soon be theirs. With glad hearts they got into the baskets and boisterously bade *Gangbo* tie them up securely and kick them into the water. *Gangbo* tied up the baskets one by one firmly and finally rolled them all into the water. *Gangbo* went back to the village and took possession of the villagers' land and property and made their wives and children his subjects. He grew rich and powerful and lived happily afterwards.

4.4.2. *Awat and Matchadus*[23]

There is a division of hill tribe people, known as *Matchadu* or *Dudurong*, in the north-eastern region of India, who have in their long-guarded possession their own distinct anciently inherited Psycho-Physical Secrets. The anciently-inherited

---

[23] The *matchadu* or *dudurong* is a tiger man. Every day, in unearthly hours of night, every *matchadu*, physically metamorphosed into a tiger, prowls about in the deep jungles, hunts for wild pigs, deer, bison and other animals and also catches fish in the streams, rivers, ponds and lakes. Just when it is darkest before dawn each day, the metamorphosed tiger is transformed into a human being.

primitive secret psycho-physical culture, whereby one is physically transformed into a tiger at dusk, when the shade of night falls is a distinctive prorogation of a segment of the Hill People, known as *Matchadus* or *Dudurongs*. Every day, as the shades of night fall, each *matchadu* gets ready to undergo the routine ordeal of physical metamorphosis into a tiger (Rongmuthu, 2011, 118).

Once in very ancient days, there was a little colony of *matchadus*, a race of black mop-headed cannibals, who were half-men and half-tigers. The *matchadus* generally assumed the shapes of men and dressed themselves in clothing like human beings. By this means they used to decoy men and women and devour them. One day, intrepid *Awat* (a young man) filled a large basket with sweet scented *monaretchi* (banana fibre) and carried them to sell at the colony of *matchadus*. On his arrival, *Awat* generously distributed the sweet bananas free to all *matchadus*. After they had eaten, *Awat* asked them fearlessly how they liked the bananas. They discourteously ignored his question instead they asked *Awat* 'where does the fruit which you have brought grow? On a vine or a tree?' *Awat* answered that it grew on a big tall tree. Then the *matchadus* forced *Awat* to show them the coveted tree. But before leading them away, the adventurous young man warned them of an impending attack and told them to bring out all their money, valuable gongs, precious beads and clothes from their homes and conceal them in a cave near their colony. Then, after removing their valuables, *Awat* asked them to put their wives and children inside their houses and fasten the doors from outside. So when the thieves come to their colony, they would hear the voices from within the houses and run away. The *matchadus* did exactly as advised by *Awat*. Then the grown up male members of the *matchadus* joyfully ambled after *Awat* in blissful anticipation of the fruit which would soon be theirs. *Awat* led them to a gigantic *simul* tree (bombax malabaricum), the circumference of which was fifty cubits and the branches of which were heavily laden with half-ripening bolls of cotton. *Awat* told them to squat together on the ground near the tree and wait while he cut down the tree for them with his axe.

Awat cut the tree in such a way as to let it fall on them all. When it was about to topple, he shouted aloud, "now look up at the tree and stretch your hands aloft to get the fruits" (Rongmuthu, 2008, 97 - 98). All the *matchadus* in close concourse raised their outstretched hands towards the falling tree. When it fell with a tremendous crash, the tree instantaneously killed all the assembled *matchadus. Awat* speedily returned to their colony and set their houses on fire. All the female *matchadus* with their young children were burnt alive. After this, *Awat* returned to his own village bringing with him all the money, valuable gongs, precious beads and clothes. He made himself the sole possessor of the *matchadus'* wealth.

4.4.3. *Jereng,* the orphan[24]

Jereng an orphan boy, lived in a village, he was about five summers old. He had no other relations to turn to for help; and as no one in the village could look after him or give him food, he decided to enter the forest himself in search of wild fruits and edible roots. While *Jereng* was on the tree eating and enjoying himself, a pair of terrible cannibals, known as *matchadus*, came by. They espied the orphan high up on the

---

[24] This is the story of how animal trickster deceives a boy but in turn they themselves get deceived.

tree and begged him for some of the luscious fruits which he was eating. Obliging to their request, *Jereng* vigorously shook the tree, causing a shower of fruit to descend near the couple. But they failed to partake of it. Instead, they complained that the fruit had fallen on dirty ground and was polluted. They now asked him to pluck some fruit with his own hands and lower it to them by means of his toes. At first *Jereng* was suspicious of the terrible *matchadus* and would not listen to their request. However, when they assured him that no harm would come to him, the orphan half reluctantly let down some fruits with his toes. Promptly the *matchadus* seized him by the feet, pulled him down off the tree, tied him up in a cage and carried him to their home. There they had a young son of their own who was about the same age as *Jereng*. The following day, the *matchadus* said to their own child to kill the boy and cook him well for the evening meal and set off to cultivate their fields. When his parents had departed, the young *matchadu*, looking at the orphan said: "We *matchadus* are all dark-skinned. You men are fair skinned. Pray tell me how you become so?" (Rongmuthu, 2008, 100) *Jereng* answered,

> When we bathe, we do so in boiling water. If you want to be as fair as man, loosen me and I will boil water and bathe you (Rongmuthu, 2008, 100).

The young *matchadu* eagerly freed the captured boy and *Jereng* promptly began to heat some water. When it had reached the boiling point, he said to the young *matchadu* to take off his clothes and go down to the pigsty under the house and sit still there till *Jereng* poured water upon him. The unsuspecting *matchadu* youngster did as he was told. *Jereng* speedily poured the boiling water upon him, and the *matchadu* soon died of the burns which he received.

Jereng hastily clad himself in his victim's clothes, and smeared dirty, black soot all over his body until he exactly resembled the dead boy. He then cooked his body, well for the parent's meal. At dusk the mother and father returned from the fields and, without squeamishness, began to eat their evening meal which was elaborately served. After a while they remarked idly that the meat smells like the flesh of their own child. The orphan promptly replied:

> Dear parents, I killed the boy and cooked his body as you told me. Perhaps in the midst of toil in dressing the meat, a few drops of my perspiration fell into it (Rongmuthu, 2008, 101).

This silenced the hungry couple and they finished their repast without further comment. Sometime later, *Jereng* pretended to be sad. When the *matchadus* questioned him concerning his sadness, the boy said to them:

> I am your only child; you are getting old. Who knows when you will die? Yet, you have not shown me any of your wealth. Therefore, it is clear that you do not love me! (Rongmuthu, 2008, 101)

The parents, to remove his anxiety, promptly revealed to him all their possessions. The following day, when the *matchadus* left the house, the orphan hid all their money, jewels and clothes on the opposite bank of the river.

A few days later *Jereng* begged the couple to take him to the river to bathe. When they arrived there, he asked them to let him learn to swim, though in truth, the orphan was an excellent swimmer. The parents flatly refused to grant his request telling him that he would certainly be drowned. The boy would not listen to their pleas, but cried out more, until finally the *matchadus* reluctantly gave him permission to try. Whereupon the orphan adroitly leaped, into the water and swam swiftly to the other side. There he divested himself of the clothes of the dead young *matchadu* and shouted triumphantly to the parents of the dead boy:

> You *Matchadus*, have devoured your own child. Look,
> I am the child of man whom you seized by treachery.
> See, I have all your wealth and precious clothes. Your
> own iniquity overwhelms you now (Rongmuthu,
> 2008, 102).

The *matchadus* were beside themselves with rage against the insolent boy; but they could do nothing about it, since neither of them knew how to swim. The orphan cried out to them once more:

> If you want to cross the river over here, sit on the
> backs of earthen pitchers and row them on. If you
> want to cross quickly, punch holes in the pitchers
> (Rongmuthu, 2008, 102).

The gullible *matchadus* followed his advice and were consequently drowned. *Jereng* gathered up the possessions and went away from the river side.

4.4.4. The Monkey and the Tortoise

A common short tailed monkey and a tortoise were once great friends. One day they started out together with conical shaped fishing baskets made of bamboo for fishing. The monkey, being cleverer than the tortoise, reserved all the best fishing places for himself and set his baskets in them. The tortoise, being unable to secure suitable spots, took his chance and set only one single trap and that too, in a small, muddy lake where wild boars were accustomed to come and wallow. The next day a large number of fish got entrapped in the monkey's baskets; but he would not give even a small portion to the tortoise.

On a later date the tortoise went to see his basket and found a big, wild pig caught in it. He speared it and it squealed loud and long. The monkey hearing the shrill squeals of the wild pig came running to the spot, and found the pig at the point of death. He helped the tortoise kill it, keeping himself at a safe distance from the wild pig and all along merely tapping it with the tip of a long bamboo pole. The tortoise was about to take the body of the wild pig in a lump to the house. But the monkey suggested to cut the body into pieces and to take only the good portions of the flesh. The monkey also said that they better cook the meat there itself and take it home later.

The simple tortoise assented to his proposal. So they cut the meat into joints and steaks, dried and smoked them and cooked the best pieces on the spot. Then the monkey said:

> Let us enjoy this cooked meat together on the top
> of a big tree on yonder hill. From there we can get
> a wonderful view of our motherland while we are
> eating (Rongmuthu, 2008, 138).

The tortoise said that he could not climb trees. Together they carried the cooked meat to the foot of a big tree on a hill. The monkey said, "Let me first take the meat up the tree. When it is all up, I shall hoist you" (Rongmuthu, 2008, 138). Again the poor tortoise consented and they worked together to get the cooked meat to the top of a tall tree. When it was all there, the monkey told the tortoise to catch hold of his tail with his mouth. The tortoise did so. The monkey then assayed to carry him to the top; but when they were half way up the first branch, he cried out: "Alas, my tail is becoming detached. Let free your grip or we shall both die" (Rongmuthu, 2008, 139). The tortoise loosened his hold and fell heavily to the ground. Three times more the monkey tried to hoist the tortoise up the tree, but each time he pretended that his tail was coming off and the simple tortoise fell to the ground with a heavy thud. At last the monkey told the tortoise to remain at the foot of the tree and that he would toss down the tortoise's share.

The tortoise stayed at the foot of the tree and the monkey scrambled up the tree and threw down only the bones from which he had already cleaned the meat. In anger the duped tortoise went to the river and meditated revenge and waited for his deceitful friend. In the evening the monkey came down to the river for a drink. As he was bending over the water, the tortoise grabbed the lower portion of his buttocks with his strong jaws. The monkey screamed in excruciating pain and implored the tortoise to set him free; but the later would not listen. So, wherever he went, the monkey had to carry the tortoise with him.

4.4.5. *Mikkol*[25]

In a certain village there lived two beautiful sisters named *Nose* and *Dimse*. One day they took their *koksi* (woven bamboo basket to catch fish, prawns, crabs, cockles

---

[25] *Mikkol* - name of the infatuated monkey. His name is suggestive of his physiological simian heritage. *Mik* stands for eye and *kol* for hole or depression. Evidently it suggests the depression-like eye sockets of the monkey.

and small fish etc) and *chekke* (coop like nets made from slit bamboo especially meant for catching prawns, crabs and small fish) and went upstream looking for small fry and prawns. *Mikkol*, a short tailed monkey, spotted them and fell in love instantly. Immediately he began to look for ways to make the maidens reciprocate his feelings. Upstream, a group of young men were cutting bamboo to build a bachelor's dormitory; they were at the same time competing with each other as to carve the bamboo in the most artistic way. Very soon they floated down the stream several pieces of artistically cut and carved bamboo and returned home. *Mikkol* spotted the carved bamboos and thought that they could be his chance. He thought that perhaps *Nose* and *Dimse* would like them and he schemed and waited. It did not take long for the sisters to catch sight of the wonderfully carved bamboo and to fall in love with them. They began to urge each other to pick them up, saying that the bamboos were beautifully and wonderfully carved. They wanted to take them for their younger siblings at home. As they were competing with each other to pick them up, they heard a voice saying:

> Take them if you mean to take me as your husband;
> take it, if you intend to bed with me (Dhoronsing Sangma, 1988, 33).

The sisters at once directed their gaze towards the voice coming to them and realized that their object of desire was *mikkol's* handiwork and despising said '*Tuai*! *Tuai*! (an act and sound of spitting to show one's contempt) We will neither take your cut bamboos nor take you for a husband,' they spat their rejection outright, crying that it was only *mikkol*. *Mikkol* was ashamed and was left alone by the sisters.

Mikkol was not one to give up. He followed them unashamedly close on their heels. The sisters continued to fish and look for prawns upstream and covered one pool after the other. As they continued, *Dimse* caught sight of a nest full of *salchame* chicks (a kind of wild bird) in the hollow of a tree. She expressed great desire to have the chicks, saying they must be lovely. The older sibling agreed that they must be lovely indeed. It would be a nice pet for the brothers and sisters back home. *Nose,* then declared that she would marry anyone if he is able to bring down the birds for them, even if he happened to be a lean-legged *banggal* or sharp nosed *rori* (a term used by *A·chiks* to refer to non-tribals). When *mikkol* heard the declaration his joy knew no bounds. He began to pat his bottom and hop around and asked: "If I bring down the chicks, would you both take me as your husband?" "Yes", they replied "We would consider you as our beau even if you were a monkey. We would take you for a husband even if you were an ape" (Dhoronsing Sangma, 1988, 33).

No sooner had they said 'yes', he whipped into the tree and pushed his right-hand into the nest through the hollow. However, even before he could grasp any of the chicks, his hand got stuck in the hollow. He could neither push his hand in nor pull it out. 'How many chicks are there, darling *mikkol*?' asked *Nose.* 'Enough for you and me and for your brothers and sisters,' *mikkol* answered. Then *Dimse* urged him to count and say the exact number.

He began to count the chicks saying 'One, two, three, four, five, six...' The sisters below were anxious for a glimpse of the young birds. But the monkey was not able to pull out his hand, and to hide his embarrassment he pretended to count over and over again. The sisters strained their necks and waited patiently, but in vain! Ultimately they saw what had happened and cried out that *mikkol's* hand had got caught in the tree-hollow.

Yet *mikkol* would not concede defeat, he held out his left hand, waved it gloriously and declared: 'See, its here!' In the meantime *mikkol's* right hand had swelled badly. *Nose*, once again declared that *mikkol's* hand was stuck; and once again *mikkol* denied it and showed off his left hand. The sisters waited patiently till the sun was beginning to sink in the west. Ultimately the sisters refused to be taken for a ride any longer. They left him with his right hand stuck in the hollow of the tree. *Mikkol* was ashamed and helplessly watched them leave. Now *mikkol* came to realise his own mistake and began to weep for it.

Mikkol's hand was caught in the tree hollow. With no help coming from any quarter, *mikkol* bore the agony. Then on the third day a pair of cannibals, known as *matchadus* came by the spot, very close to where *mikkol* was stuck. They had come to clear a small opening in their intended *jhum* field to see if it augured well. As was the custom among *A·chik jhum* cultivators, the old *matchadu* had come to perform the *o·pata* ritual (ritual performed to appeal to *Abet Rangge* to vacate particular spot for cultivation). He cried out thus: "*Abet Rangge* (God of forests and springs) we are about to cut down the forest and disturb your dwelling; hold the blind by the hand, bear the lame in the *kok* (bamboo basket) and cross over to the other side" (Dhoronsing Sangma, 1988, 35). Hearing this *mikkol* answered: "I will not give up my motherland. I will not leave the orchard and my ancestral property" (Dhoronsing Sangma, 1988, 35). The old *matchadu* wondered if the speaker was a man or a spirit. He then trailed the sound of the voice and further down found *mikkol* hugging the tree trunk. "O, its you, ape; I will take you home and cook a dish out of you," said the *matchadu* and climbed the tree to the spot where *mikkol* was stuck.

Seeing the *matchadu*, *mikkol* quickly tried to negotiate his way out: "Its grandpa and grandma! I was joking, as I thought you to be someone else. Please forgive me. Please do not eat me up." The monkey then begged them to save him from his sorry plight and assured them that he would toil and look after them as their own son. Seeing the state that *mikkol* was in and considering their own childlessness, the *matchadu* maneuvered the tree hollow with his axe and put an end to the monkey's sufferings. Thus freed, *mikkol* now followed his just adopted grandparents to their home, where his injured hand was tended to and cared for in the best possible way. *Mikkol*'s swollen hand improved and one day *mikkol* told his grandparents:

> Grandpa, Grandma, it's you who are my parents, for; had you not rescued me I was as good as dead. Seeing that you have saved me from death I am greatly indebted to you. Now, I will do all the work for you; you sit, eat and live as kings and queens do. I will clear the land, do the farming, build houses for you; you just relax, I will even fetch water for you to wash yourselves at home. I will look after you and provide for you till you die. Tomorrow I mean to start clearing the land for cultivation like everyone else. Do prepare a midday meal for me (Sangma Dhoronsing, 1988, 35).

Morning came and the old *matchadu*'s wife gave *mikkol* a food packet for his midday meal. *Mikkol* started alone for the *jhum* field with his headgear well placed and the machete sticking out from his armpit. However, on reaching the hill intended to be the *jhum* field, he chose a comfortable branch and settled down there and intoned: 'Let the young bamboo from the *jhum* fringe bend over, bend over; and let this hand of mine, grow anew, grow anew' for his hand had decomposed and fallen off. When he was hungry he ate the food that he carried and whiled away his time. It was only when evening set in that he jumped from tree to tree and worked himself up to sweat and tiredness and went back home. Once home, after supper *mikkol* informed his grandparents that his farm was going to be better than anyone else's. The *matchadu* couples were happy thinking that *mikkol* was dedicating himself to work with all his might.

When the time came for the burning of the *jhum* field, *mikkol* reminded his grandparents to get the seeds ready. He then pretended to proceed towards the *jhum* field when in reality he only whiled away his time watching the others burning their *jhum* fields. In the evening he worked himself up to a sweat by hopping from one tree to another and returned home. He told the grandparents that in his village, they boiled corn, yam and all the seeds whole night before planting.

The grandma thought this to be true and boiled the seeds the whole night. *Mikkol* got up early in the morning, placed his midday meal and the boiled seeds in the basket and went to the field. The old couple wanted to go and help *mikkol* with the sowing. But *mikkol* declined their help. He went alone, and as he was far off, intending a great leisure, he looked for a breezy spot under a tree and ate the boiled seeds. He even slept wherever he wanted to. Only when the evening set, he covered himself with soot and returned home. In this way *mikkol* continued to deceive the old couple every day.

However, a day came when the *matchadu* and his wife would no longer be denied a glimpse of their *jhum* field. Finding no way out *mikkol* assured them to take them the next day. That day, reaching the *jhum* area, *mikkol* selected the spot that was best scorched by the flames and did a little more of clearing and planted wild grasses, wild oats and yams.

Back home in the evening *mikkol* boasted that his grandparents had done well by listening to him when he told them about sowing seeds pre-boiled. He, then proudly informed them that his rice, corn, yam and other plants have grown better and faster than those in other fields. *Mikkol* had a particular view point in mind and thither he took the old couple. From a vantage point on a rock he told them to look yonder towards the hill that he had earlier filled with wild plants. The couple looked and found that their *jhum* field appeared to be more luxuriant than those around it. They were satisfied for the time being. *Mikkol* urged them to go on their own to the *jhum* field. They moved on and reached the indicated spot. Soon they realized that the field was but filled with wild grass, wild oats and wild yams.

At last it dawned on the old couple that they had been tricked! And when *mikkol* realized that he had been exposed, he clambered onto a tree. From the safety of the treetop *mikkol* cried out that the old couple was such helplessly gullible creatures! He also confessed to them that he had eaten away the boiled seeds all day long, sitting on a rock. He then laughed at them. The old *matchadu* couple was very angry yet helpless and returned home.

The old *matchadu* and his wife, then, began to think of ways of paying back *mikkol* with the same coin. Before long they had a plan. They conferred with the villagers and asked them to help catch *mikkol*. The villagers consented to help.

One day the *matchadu* and his wife pretended to be dead and the whole village played along and mourned for them. The *do·mesal* (species of wild fowl) was sent to convey the sad news to *mikkol*. *Do·mesal* went to the dwelling place of *mikkol* and told him that his grandfather and grandmother had stopped eating and drinking since he left them. They got sick due to lack of food and eventually had died. And the villagers had sent the *do·mesal* to fetch him thinking that he may wish to see their faces for one last time. But *mikkol* replied: 'I know you are lying. They mean to eat me up.' The *do·mesal* tried to convince the monkey saying: 'No I am not lying to you. You should see how everyone in the village is crying and mourning for them. You can come and see at least from the treetop.' But *mikkol* would not be convinced and saying that he could detect no sign of grief in the *do·mesal*, he ran away. The *do·mesal* returned unsuccessful.

After this, the *do·grik* (black pheasant) was sent to convey the sad news to *mikkol*. The bird flew up to the monkey and tried to make him believe that his grandparents had died by telling him a good number of things. But *mikkol* would not believe him also. At last the pheasant said: 'I've just come from mourning for them, look at my eyes: they're swollen.' It proved very convenient that the *do·grik* had eyes that were naturally red in colour. *Mikkol* looked at the bird's eyes and believed it. *Mikkol* began to cry exclaiming: "O Grandpa, O Grandma, you died because you could not live without me" (Dhoronsing Sangma, 1988, 40). The *do·grik* then pointed out that it was no use crying far away in the forest, but that he should go and express his sorrow in their house. *Mikkol* complied.

As he neared the village, *mikkol* was filled with mixed feelings of fear and boldness. From a distance *mikkol* saw that the *matchadu*'s house was crowded with people and did not doubt any longer. With renewed courage he walked into the yard, squatted on the ground and began to cry calling out for his grandparents. Then the crowd reprimanded him saying: "If you really loved your grandparents you should enter the house and mourn there" (Dhoronsing Sangma, 1988, 40).

So *mikkol* ventured as far as the verandah. As *mikkol* entered the house, the drummers and other musicians began to beat the drums to indicate: "Shut the door, lock the back door, block the holes, and block the holes." Then again the crowd said: "If you really love your grandparents, go and sit by their head and cry for them" (Dhoronsing Sangma, 1988, 41).

Accordingly *mikkol* rose and began to caress his grandparents and cry for them. As *mikkol* was crying in this manner, the *matchadu* and his wife caught *mikkol* by his wrist and said: "Ha, now, we got you. You have deceived us greatly and now you will have to die." *Mikkol* begged for forgiveness but the old couple did not relent. Thus *mikkol* died (Dhoronsing Sangma, 1988, 41).

The above examples show some of the common characteristics of trickster figure, as the trickster are ambiguous and anomalous. They are tricky mythical beings likely enough to entice any human mind. They are performers of heroic acts on behalf of men, yet in their original form, or in some later form, foolish, obscene, laughable yet indomitable. He is incarnated as a clever, mischievous man or creature who tries to survive the dangers and challenges of the world using trickery and deceit as a defense.

The trickster is a deceiver and trick player such as *Gangbo nokma*, *Jereng*, *Mikkol* and the *Matchadu*. The trickster uses trickery to bring about the change he is targeting. He gets tricked by his own nature. It is his misguided ambitions, his poor control of himself and his desires that lead him into situations where his lack of control continually makes him fail or become duped himself. He possesses no values, moral or social; he is at the mercy of his passions and appetites. The *mikkol* (monkey) is the example of such traits.

The trickster is a shape-shifter. The trickster can alter his shape of bodily appearance in order to facilitate deception. The trickster may change form, sex, and so forth as an element of surprise to his victim. Trickster is amoral and likes change; he does not care what effect it has or what consequences follow in its wake. *Gangbo nokma*'s trickery caused the death of the villagers, *Awat* and *Jereng* showed similar cruelty.

Like *Gangbo nokma* the trickster is a situation inventor, he can turn a bad situation into a good one, and then back into a bad one. The trickster can often turn any situation to his advantage, despite the odds against him. The trickster is a sacred and lewd bricoleur, he manifests a distinctive transformative ability: he can find the lewd in the sacred and the sacred in the lewd and new life from both. The trickster may be idealized as a cultural hero when, as the agent of transformation, he overturns a cruel or unfair leader or political/social system or reverses the fortunes of the more powerful party. For example Prometheus, Raven, and Maui steal fire from the gods and give it to humans. In that the *A·chik* trickster too are often cited as examples of social ethics and survival propriety.

The trickster is often portrayed as a much weaker character than his prey such as *Gangbo nokma*, or *Jereng* or *Awat*, and yet through cleverness and trickery, he is able to overcome all obstacles and prevail. In some cases the trickster may appear to be physically weaker, in order to confuse his prey (false frailty).

Conclusion

Jean L. Mercier in his book, *Being Human* (1998), writes that the human person is a conscious being in the world. Our humanity is never a finished product for we are sojourners in this world. We have an aim to pursue in freedom, which never ends in this world. We are free persons not for nothing but for a purpose (1998, 62-63).

Abrams' understanding of the term 'folklore' implies the sayings, verbal compositions, and social rituals that are handed down mostly orally and not necessarily in written form. Therefore, folklore includes legends, superstitions, songs, tales, proverbs, riddles, spells, and the like. Morrison, on the other hand, said that all societies have a history and all history begins as oral. Presently it offers a challenge to the accepted myths of history. With complete reliance on the written document, the paradigm of history becomes inevitably a prisoner of the idiosyncratic written testimony that has been created to survive.

Historians claim that history is an ongoing process which involves a dialogue between the present and the past in order to understand the future. Hence, when one of the elements is presented falsely, it automatically affects all. Folk narratives include many other categories of oral lore which has its own manifold distinctions like myth, fairy tale or *marchen*, romantic tale or novella, religious tale, folktale, legend, animal tale, anecdote, joke, numskull tale, etc. Besides, proverbs and riddles are also important parts of oral literature.

The religious aspect of social folk customs in India is multidimensional and highly complex. Many tribal groups do not maintain close contacts with the firmly established mainstream religious practices but the maintenance of indigenous modes of worship have been preserved carefully. The *human* element in narrative is important. We can say here that narrative must have a *human* agent who must do something, or something must be done to him or her. The *human* factor can be regarded as a *paradigmatic core feature* of the narrative.

Klaus Roth summarized that narratives play a role in and for intercultural communication by the representation and revelation of the image of other cultures, playing a role in the actual communicative acts between people from different cultures, using it for the communication of cultural contacts and conflicts, and playing a role in the teaching of intercultural competence.

One of the basic purposes of narrative is to entertain, to gain and hold a readers' interest. As far as development or modernization is concerned, the *A·chik* society has largely remained traditional rather than 'modern'. The common *A·chik* folk have retained the century old intimacy with their tribal life world.

The *A·chiks* are very religious and god-fearing people. They believe that all physical ailments, accidents and unnatural deaths are due to the wrath of one or the other malevolent spirits. Therefore, sacrifices of animals and birds must be offered to the deities to appease them as well as to invoke their blessings (Milton Sangma, 1981, 233). It is noteworthy that the indispensable function which myths fulfill in primitive cultures is to express, enhance and codify belief, to safeguard and enforce morality, to vouch for the efficiency of the ritual and to contain practical rules for the guidance of man. Thus myth is a force that helps to maintain society itself; therefore, myth and religion as a whole continue to play an important part in social life.

Myths have a sacred quality and the sacred communication is made in symbolic form. The myth of concern comprises everything that a society is most concerned to know. Frye is of the opinion that a myth of concern has its roots in religion and only later branches out into politics, law and literature. It is inherently traditional and conservative, placing a strong emphasis on values of coherence and continuity. Schorer opined that myths were the instruments by which we continually struggle to make our experience intelligible to ourselves. Wheelwright explains how myth is the expression of a profound sense of togetherness of feeling and of action and of wholeness of living. In other words, myths never remain static, as they are continually retold and rewritten; and in this process they are constantly modulated and transformed.

Malinowski explains how myth is a vital ingredient of human civilization; it is not an ideal tale, but an active force; it is not an intellectual explanation or an artistic imagery, but a pragmatic charter of primitive faith and moral wisdom (1976, 785).

The word 'myth' may mean 'sacred story', 'traditional story', or 'story involving gods', but it does not mean 'false story'. Therefore, many scholars refer to a religious stories as 'myths' without intending to offend members of that religion. Religion begins with a sense of wonder and awe and the attempt to tell stories that will connect us to God. Then it becomes a set of theological works in which everything is reduced to a code, to a creed. Religion turns poetry to prose

(Campbell, *et al*, 1991, 173-74). Nevertheless; this scholarly use of the word 'myth' may cause misunderstanding and offend people who cherish those myths. This is because word 'myth' is popularly used to mean 'falsehood'. Many myths, such as ritual myths, are clearly part of religion. However, unless we simply define myths as 'sacred stories', not all myths are necessarily religious.

It may be concluded therefore that the formation of myth is subject to certain laws and not due to an arbitrary exercise of the imagination. When history is telescoped into myth, the myth maker always has the objective of bringing out certain features deeply characteristic of human behaviour. The myth-maker feels free to select his facts from a wide sphere; he is not concerned with the literal truth of his story; but with linking facts chosen from a vast field of events into a significant whole, a concrete universal story.

It is a concrete story about certain people with definite names and about certain events in definite places. But it is a universal story in that it portrays the most universal patterns of human life, such as motherhood, fatherhood, elemental envy or devotion.

Although there is no specific universal myth, there are many themes and motifs that recur in the myths of various cultures and ages. Some cultures have myths of the creation of the world; these range from a god fashioning the earth from abstract chaos to a specific animal creating it from a handful of mud. Certain other cultures were concerned with longer periods of vegetative death through prolonged drought. Myths treating the origin of fire, or its retrieval from some being who has stolen it or refused to share it; the millennium to come; and the dead or the relation between the living and the dead, are common.

Archetypes, on the other hand, are elementary ideas, what could be called 'ground' ideas. Jung spoke of these ideas as archetype of the unconscious which implies that it comes from below and is biologically grounded (see Campbell, *et al*, 1991, 60-61).

Archetypes form a dynamic substratum common to all humanity, upon the foundation of which each individual builds his own experience of life, developing a unique array of psychological characteristics. Archetype has its sources in anthropology and in Jungian theory. An archetype is the first real example or prototype of something. In this sense an archetype can be considered the ideal model, the supreme type or the perfect image of something.

Archetypes determine the form of imagery, rather than content. They are inferred from the vast range of concrete images and symbols found in mythologies, religions, dreams and art across history and space. An archetype appears in myths, but can also be seen in its thematic or figurative dimension in literature, involving exile, rebirth, earth, goddess, etc.

All the most powerful ideas in history go back to archetypes. This is particularly true of religious ideas, but the central concepts of science, philosophy, and ethics are no exception to this rule. In their present form they are variants of archetypal ideas created by consciously applying and adapting these ideas to reality. For it is the function of consciousness not only to recognize and assimilate the external world through the gateway of the senses, but also to translate the world within us into visible reality.

There are so many elements and patterns which form the narrative of the folk literature of the *A·chiks*. Most of these narratives are in oral form and they continue to survive down the generations being alive only through oral renditions and community memories. Interestingly, these narratives have significantly shaped and governed the cultural consciousness of the *A·chiks*. The *A·chiks*, being a community with intimate proximity to nature and its mystical manifestations, invented a rich heritage of folklore and narratives by aligning the mystical as well as the innocent and the experiential comprehension of their immediate reality into the folk narratives that matured with time into abiding community beliefs.

Various aspects of the *A·chik* tradition that have rich and diverse cultural heritage are reflected in the folk narratives of *Krita—amua, Dani, Ajea, Grapmangtata* or *Kabe* or *Grapmikchi, Doroa, Do·sia, Katta Agana, Salling* or *Katta Salling,* etc. For the *A·chiks*, folk songs like *Nanggore* are intrinsic and inseparable parts of culture. Marked with diversity and versatility in composition and melody, songs remain ingrained in the day to day life of the *A·chiks*.

Myths and archetypes, in fact, form an essential part of the folklore of the *A·chiks*. The *A·chiks* have developed a rich storehouse of folklore. *A·chik* myths and archetypes are those connected with rivers and the physical features of the lands they settled in. Archetypes occur in different times and places in myth, literature, folklore and rituals. They have woven myths and archetypes around mystic and mysterious physical phenomena like that of the rivers, clouds, the thunder, lightning, the sun and stars, the hills and other natural formations to give plausible and imaginative explanations of their origin and existence, adding more mystery to them in the process. An element of reverence and fear can be traced in those myths. Myths make a large part of the thematic content of their oral narratives and poetry. Myths serve to explain the intentions and actions of supernatural beings. Most myths are concerned with religion, which involve rituals and prescribed forms of sacred ceremonies. Some of the recurring myths that have a strong presence in the cultural narratives of the *A·chiks* are associated with places like *Balpakram*, with rivers like *Songdu* (Brahmaputra) like *Dura A·bri*, *Rangira*, with spirits, mountains, with ideas of reincarnations, the whirlpools as in *Tematchi Wari* (in Ildek river), *Mrik Wari* (in *Simsang* river), *Dombe Wari* and many more.

As mentioned already, the four types of Archetypes by Jung are mother archetypes, forms relating to rebirth, spirits and trickster figures. These archetypes of Jung can be traced in *A·chik* folk narratives. It is found that the mother archetype appears under an almost infinite variety of aspects. Mythology offers many variations of the mother archetype. Besides, the river forms a major theme in *A·chik* folk narrative mostly symbolizing fertility as well as motherhood. The rivers are also shown as enduring symbols of the passage of time. It also highlights the conception of a river as the source of the origin, evolution and growth of human civilization.

Garo Hills is blessed with rivers, lakes and streams making the land fertile and the naturally available items of food are found in abundance. In the early days people never went hungry because they knew how to use nature and live with it. Abundant flora and fauna adorned the entire hills and mountains of Garo Hills and the people living therein (Julius Marak, 2004, 154). Earlier *A·chik* villages were located near some streams or waterfalls.

The present study shows as to how the concept of rebirth forms the second category of archetype in *A·chik* tradition and that it has various aspects, which is not always used in the same sense. Jung enumerates mainly the following different forms of rebirth namely:

Metempsychosis or transmigration of souls; Reincarnations; Rebirth (Renovatio) and Transformation.

In *Balpakram: The Land of the Spirits,* Julius R. Marak affirms that the *A·chiks* have a strong belief in the Kingdom of God. The *A·chiks* believed that in *Chitmang* Hill lived a god almighty who was the giver of human lives. Metempsychosis or transmigration of souls indicates that one's life is prolonged in time by passing through different bodily existences or from another point of view, it is a life sequence interrupted by different reincarnations. Similarly, the *A·chiks* too believe in the transmigration of souls. Reincarnation as a concept of rebirth necessarily implies the continuity of a personality. Here the human personality is regarded as continuous and accessible to memory so that when one is reincarnated or born, one is able, at least potentially; to remember that one has lived through previous existences and these existences were one's own, that is, they had the same ego form as the present life.

The phenomenology of the spirit in fairytales involves the third category of Jungian archetype, that is, transformation. The *A·chiks* believe in the existence of a Supreme Deity who is sometimes identified as *Tatara Rabuga*. He is the greatest of all the deities and spirits of the *A·chik* pantheon. It is also interesting to note that the trickster plays an important role in *A·chik* tradition. The trickster is an object of study in mythology, religion, anthropology, psychology, and recently in film as well. The trickster is a divinity or semi-divine creature that pops up in almost every mythology or folklore of the world. It is the god of the crossroads, or of trade, of mischief, the physical representation of randomness, and an agent of chaos.

However, the traditional *A·chik* culture is in the process of constant transformation. The rise and spread of the TV phenomenon in India has been very fast. It has made a strong impact on Indian society and mass culture. The TV advertising is another area in which folklore metaphors, symbols, designs, motifs, and ideas are transformed to popularize or boost the modern industrial products, and as such become an important part of mass culture. The impact of popular media in *A·chik* society provides a potential area of further research engagement.

Indian folklorists have traditionally been searching for folk elements in modern cultural expressions like literature, painting, and art for instance. But they have not yet tried their tools on other kind of contemporary expressions such as films, advertisement, mass media, folk speech, particularly slang, commercial products and other forms of Indian mass culture (Handoo, 2000, 216).

Technological innovations have radically changed our lives and it could be looked upon as a gift to mankind from god or at least as divine. Folk narratives show that new technology has very often been understood as an extension of pre-technological culture. Modernization, new technology and innovations gave rise to new folklore and new traditions. Mass Media, for example, was at first seen as destroying the 'purity' of folklore and oral tradition, but it was soon realized that mass media in fact was becoming a new carrier of folklore and oral tradition. The mass entertainment industry did not become a one way communication, but broadened the horizons of folklore and oral tradition in the modern times.

The study of folklore in contemporary society ought to include the relations of folklore and mass media on different levels and in various ways. Folklore is a dynamic component of culture which functions adaptively in situations of rapid cultural change.

Folklore and tradition have always implied change and continuity. According to Gary Alan Fine, "Folklorists should treasure the proverb that 'the more things change, the more things remain the same'" (Fine, Gary Alan, 1985, 41: 7). The 'modernization' of the societies led many scholars to believe that "folklore was dying or would die out very soon. And in fact some genres did disappear from oral tradition due to the impact of the modernization, but they continued to live on in the other forms of modern media" (Handoo, *et al*, 1999, 1-7). "Television," writes Gary Alan Fine, "has apparently changed the temporal boundaries of entertainment, possibly more than it has altered the content of the stories" (Fine, Gary Alan, 1985:8).

Folklore as a discipline at the end of the millennium faces new challenges. All disciplines are challenged from time to time to accommodate new knowledge, new ideas and new theories for new needs and even new functions of the discipline and to discard what had become obsolete and irrelevant. These challenges in fact revitalize disciplines and there are no permanent frameworks or permanent theories or methods in any dynamic discipline. J.G. Frazer as early as 1935 explained this phenomenon very appropriately:

> A superstructure theory is always transitory, being constantly superseded by fresh theories which make nearer and nearer approaches to the truth without ever reaching it. On the shore of the great ocean of reality men are perpetually building theoretical castles of sand, which are perpetually being washed away by the rising tide of knowledge... (Frazer, 1935, viii)

Select Bibliography

Abbott, H. Porter. *The Cambridge Introduction to Narrative*. Cambridge: University Press, 2002. Print.

Abrams, M.H. *A Glossary of Literary Terms* (2nd Indian Reprint). India: Akash Press, 2008. Print.

Almen, Byron. "Narrative Archetypes: A Critique, Theory, and Method of Narrative Analysis". *Journal of Music Theory* 47. 1 (Spring, 2003):1-39. Duke University Press on behalf of the Yale University Department of Music, *JSTOR*. Web 17 Feb. 2009.

Bal, Mieke. *Narratology: Introduction to the Theory of Narratives*. trans. by C. Van Boheemen, 1st ed. London: University of Toronto Press, 1985. Print.

-----.*Introduction to the Theory of Narrative*. (Toronto, Buffalo), London: University of Toronto Press, 1997. Print.

Baron, Robert and Nicholas Spitzer. "Introduction" *In Public Folklore*. eds. Robert Baron and Nicholas Spitzer. Washington, London: Smithsonian Institute Press, 1992. Print.

Barthes, Ronald. *Introduction to the Structural Analysis of Narratives*, in Image-Music-Text. ed. and trans,

Stephen Heath. New York: Hill and Wang, 1977. Print.

-----. *Mythologies*, London: Paladin, 1973. Print.

Barthes, Ronald and Lionel Duisit. "An Introduction to the Structural Analysis of Narrative". *New Literary History* 6.2 (Winter, 1975): 237-272. The John Hopkins University Press, *JSTOR*. 1ˢᵗ Org/stable/468419. Web 18 Aug. 2008.

Bascom, William R. "Folklore and Anthropology". *Journal of American Folklore* 66 (1953): 283 -90. Print.

-----. "Verbal Art". *Journal of American Folklore* 68 (1955): 245-52. Print.

Bausinger, Hermann. "Media, Technology and Daily Life". *Media, Culture and Society.* 6 (1984): 343-51. Print.

Ben Amos, Dan. "Toward a Definition of Folklore in Context". *The Journal of American Folklore* 84.331(Jan-Mar., 1971): Toward a New Perspective in Folklore 3-15, *JSTOR*. Org/ sici – Web. 26 March 2012.

Ben Amos, Dan and Keneth S.Goldstein. *Folklore: Performance and Communication.* Mouton – The Hague, Paris, 1975. Print.

Bhattacharjee, Jayanta Bhusan. *The Garos and the English 1765-1874.* New Delhi: Radiant Publishers, 1978. Print.

Broner, Simon J. *The Meaning of Folklore: The Analytical Essays of Alan Dundes.* Logan: Utah State University, All USU Press Publication, 2007. Print.

Brooks, Peter. *Psychoanalysis and Storytelling*. Oxford: Blackwell, 1994. Print.

-----. *The Law as Narrative and Rhetoric*. In Peter Brooks and Paul Gewirtz (eds.), Law's Stories: Narrative and Rhetoric in the Law. New Haven: Yale University Press, 1996. Print.

Buck, M. Harry Jr. "From History to Myth: A comparative Study". *Journal of Bible and Religion* 29.3 (July, 1961): 219-226. Oxford University Press, *JSTOR*. Web 17 Feb. 2009.

Burling, Robbins. *Rengsanggri – Family and Kingship of a Garo Village* (2nd Edition). Tura: Tura Book Room, 1997. Print.

Burton, Richard. *Arabian Nights*. New York: Cosimo. Inc., 1932. Print.

Campbell, Joseph. *The Masks of God: Primitive Mythology*. London: Martin Secker and Warburg, 1960. Print.

-----. *Myth and Meaning in Contemporary Times*. Joseph Campbell Foundation. www.worldchanges.com/html. Web 24 May, 2012.

Campbell, Joseph with Bill Moyers. *The Power of Myth*. ed. Flowers Betty Sue. New York: A Division of Random House, INC, 1991. Print.

Carey, William. *The Garo Jungle Book* (2nd Edition). Tura: Tura Book Room, 1993. Print.

Carroll, Michael P. "Levi-Strauss, Freud, and the Trickster: A New Perspective upon an Old Problem". *American Ethnologist* 8. 2 (May, 1981): 301-313. Blackwell Publishing on behalf of the American Anthropologist Association, *JSTOR*. Web 17 Feb. 2009.

Chatman, Seymour. *Story and Discourse*. Ithaca, New York: Cornell University Press, 1978. Print.

Chattopadhyay, S.K and M.S. Sangma. *The Garo Customary Laws*. Shillong: Directorate of Arts and Culture, Meghalaya, 1989. Print.

Choudhury, Nishipada Dev. "Role of Rivers for the Development of Civilization with special Reference to the History and Culture of Garo Hills, Meghalaya"; *Rivers and Culture: Focus on Garo Hills*. eds. Marak R Caroline and Sujit Som, Bhopal: IGRMS, 2004. Print.

Cohen, S Percy. "Theories of Myth". *Man*, New Series 4. 3 (Sep., 1969): 337-353. Royal Anthropological Institute of Great Britain and Ireland, *JSTOR*. Web 16 Feb. 2009.

Costa, Giulio SDB. *The Garo Code of Law*. Editor of "Anthropos", Switzerland: Posiueus (Frihourg), 1954. Print.

Denham, D Robert. *Northrop Frye on Culture and Literature* (A Collection of Review Essays). Chicago: The University of Chicago Press, 1978. Print.

De Saussure, Ferdinand. *Course in General Linguistic*. eds. by Charles Bally and Albert Sechehaye in collaboration with Albert Riedlingev. Trans. by Wade Bastain. New York: MC Graw-Hill Book Company, Toronto London, 1915. Print.

Dhavamony, Mariasusai. *Phenomenology of Religion.* Rome: Gregorian University Press, 1973. Print.

Dorson, Richard M. *In Folklore and Folklife: An Introduction.* Chicago: University of Chicago Press, 1972. Print.

Dorson, Richard. "Theories of Myth and the Folklorist". *Daedalus* 88. 2 (Spring, 1959): 280-290. Myth and Mythmaking, The MIT Press on behalf of American Academy of Arts & Sciences, *JSTOR*. Web 17 Feb. 2009. Print.

-----. "The Eclipse of Solar Mythology", *Journal of American Folklore* 68 (1955): 393-416. Print.

Doty, G. William. "Mythophiles' Dyscrasia: A Comprehensive Definition of Myth". *Journal of the American Academy of Religion* 48. 4(Dec., 1980): 531-562, Oxford University Press. Print.

Douglas, W Wallace. "The Meanings of "Myth" in Modern Criticism". *Modern Philology* 50. 4 (May, 1953): 232-242. The University of Chicago Press. Print.

Dundes, Alan. *Analytic Essays in Folklore.* The Hague, Paris: Mauton, 1975. Print

-----. *The Study of Folklore.* New Jersey: Prantice-Hall, 1965. Print.

Eliade, Mircea. *Myth and Reality*, New York: Harper and Row, The University of California, 1963. Print.

-----. *Myth* - an article *in the Encyclopedia Britannica* 15. 1969: 1134-35. Print.

-----. *Myth, Dreams and Mysteries.* Trans. Philip Mairet, New York: Harper and Row, 1967. Print.

-----. *The Sacred and the Profane: The Nature or Religion.* Trans. Willard R. Trask, New York: Harper and Row, 1961. Print.

Eliade, Mercia, Williard R Trask and Jonathan Z. Smith. *The Myth of the Eternal Return: Cosmos and History.* Bollingen Series, Princeton: Princeton University Press, 2005. Print.

Fenichel, O. *The Psychoanalytical Theory of Neurosis.* New York: Norton, 1945. Print.

Fine, Alan Gary. "*Social Change and Folklore: The Interpretation of Social Structure and Culture*". In ARV Scandinavian Yearbook of Foklore Vol. 41. eds. Bengt R. Jonson et al. Uppsala: The Royal Gustavus Adolphus Academy, 1985. Print.

Firth, R.W. *History and Traditon of Tikopia.* London: Polynesian Society, The University of Calfornia, 1961. Print.

Fiske, John. *Television Culture.* London: Metheun, 1987. Print.

-----. *Reading the Public.* Boston, 1989. Print.

Flam Aron. *Sacred Fool.* Stockholms University: Department of Cinema Studies, 2011. Print.

Frazer, James George. *Creation and Evolution in Primitive Cosmologies.* London, 1935. Print.

-----. *The Golden Bough: A Study in Magic and Religion,* Abridged edition: London: Macmillan, 1922. Print.

Frye, Northrop. "The Archetypes of Literature" *The Kenyon Review* 13.1(Winter 1951): 92-110. Kenyon College, *JSTOR.* Web 17 Feb. 2009. Print.

Gassah, L.S. *Garohills Land and the People.* New Delhi: Omsons Publications, 1984. Print.

Gennete, Gerard. *Figures III.* Paris: Seuil. In English (1980) *Narrative Discourse,* Ithaca, New York: Cornell University Press, 1972. Print.

-----. *Narrative Discourse An Essay in Method.* Trans by Jane E. Lewin, Ithaca, New York: Cornel University Press, 1983. Print.

Glassie, Henry. Folk Art. *In Folklore and Folklife: An Introduction.* ed. Richard M Dorson, Chicago: University of Chicago Press, 1972. Print.

Gomme, George L. *A Handbook of Folklore.* London: David Nutt for the Folklore Society, 1890. Print.

Goswami, Satyendra Nath. "The Role of Rivers in the Growth and Development of Culture with Special Referene to Garo Hills; *Rivers and Culture: Focus on*

Garo Hills. eds. Marak R Caroline and Sujit Som, Bhopal: IGRMS, 2004. Print.

Greenwood, Royston and C. R Hinings. "Understanding Strategic Change: The Contribution of Archetypes". *The Academy of Management Journal* 36.5 (Oct., 1993):1059-1081. Academy of Management, *JSTOR*. Web 17 Feb. 2009.

Grottaneli, Cristiano. "Nietzsche and Myth". *History of Religions* 37.1 (Aug., 1997): 3-20. The University of Chicago Press, *JSTOR*. Web 16 Feb. 2009. Print.

-----. "Discussing Theories of Myth" (Four Theories of Myth in Twentieth-Century History: Cassirer, Eliade, Levi-Strauss and Malinowski by Ivan Strenski), *History of Religions* 30.2 (Nov., 1990): 197-203, The University of Chicago Press, *JSTOR*. Web 16 Feb. 2009.

Guerin Wilfred L, Earle Labor, Lee Morgan, Jeanne C Reesman and John R Willingham. *A Handbook of Critical Approaches to Literature – 4ᵗʰ Edition*. Oxford: Oxford University Press, 1999. Print.

Gurudev, Sujata. "Literature and Rivers: A Study of Its infinite Charms"; *Rivers and Culture: Focus on Garo Hills*. eds. Marak. R Caroline and Sujit Som, Bhopal: IGRMS, 2004. Print.

Hamilton, Edith. *Mythology*. New York: Back Bay Books, 1998. Print.

Handoo, Jawaharlal, Desmond L Kharwanphlang & Sujit Som. *Folklore in Changing Times*. Bhopal: Indira Gandhi Rashtriya Manav Sangrahalaya, 2003. Print.

Handoo, Jawaharlal. *Folklore – An Introduction*. Mysore: Central Institute of Indian Languages, 1989. Print.

-----. *Current Trends in Folklore*. Mysore: University of Mysore Press, 1978. Print.

-----. *Folklore in Modern India*. Mysore: Central Institute of Indian Languages, 1998. Print.

-----. *Theoretical Essays in Indian Folklore*. Mysore: Zooni Publications, 2000. Print.

Handoo, Jawaharlal, and Reimund Kvideland. *Folklore in the Changing World*. Mysore: Zooni Publications, 1999. Print.

-----. *Folklore – New Perspectives*. Mysore: Zooni Publications, 1999. Print.

Handoo, Jawaharlal and Anna-Leena Siikala. *Folklore and Discourse*. Mysore: Zooni Publications, 1999. Print.

Hardy, Barbara. *Towards a Poetics of Fiction: An Approach through Narratives*. Novel 2, 5-14. 1968. Print.

Harwood, Frances. "Myth, Memory, and the Oral Tradition: Cicero in the Troibands". *American Anthropologist*, New Series 78.4 (Dec., 1976):783-796. Blackwell Publishing on behalf of the American Anthropological Association, *JSTOR*. Web 16 Feb. 2009.

Hassan, H Ihab. "Towards a Method of Myth". *The Journal of American Folkore* 65. 257 (Jul.-Sep., 1952): 205-215, University of Illinois Press on behalf of American Folklore Society, *JSTOR*. Web 17 Feb. 2009.

Hawes, Bess Lomax: "Happy Birthday, Dear American Folklore Society: Reflections on the Work and Mission of Folklorists" *In Public Folklore.* eds. Robert Baron and Nicholas Spitzer. Washington, London: Smithsonian Institution Press, 1992. Print.

Hunt, Margaret. *Grimms' Household Tales.* London: George Bell and Sons, York Street, 1884. Print.

Jansen, Hugh. "A Culture's stereotypes and their Expression in Folk Cliches". *Southwestern Journal of Anthropology* 13.2 (Summer, 1957): 184-200, University of New Mexico, *JSTOR*. Org/stable/3629106.

Jones, Adrian. *Meaning and the Interactive Narrative: In the context of object – oriented Interactive Cinema.* Simon Fraser University Surrey, 2000. Print.

Joshi, H.G. *Meghalaya Past and Present.* New Delhi: Mittal Publications, 2004. Print.

Jung, C. G and C. Kerenyi. *Essays on a Science of Mythology.* Trans. by R.F.C. Hull, Princeton: Princeton University Press, 1993. Print.

Jung, C. G. *The Archetypes and the Collective Unconscious* (Second Edition). ed. Sir Herbert Read, Michael Fordham, Gerard Alder, William McGuire, trans by R.F.C.

Hull. Princeton and Oxford: Princeton University Press, 1968. Print.

-----. *Four Archetypes* (from the collected works of C.G. Jung). Trans. R.F.C. Hull, Volume 9, Part I, Princeton: Princeton University Press, 1973. Print.

-----. *Psychology of the Unconscious* (3rd Print). eds. Herbert Read, Michael Fordham, Gerhard Adler and William McGuire, Princeton and Oxford: Princeton University Press, 2001. Print.

Joshi, H.G. *Meghalaya Past and Present*. New Delhi: Mittal Publications, 2004. Print.

Kar, P.C. *Glimpses of the Garos*. Tura: Garo Hills Book Emporium, 1982. Print.

Kirshenblatt-Gimblett, Barbara. "Mistaken Dichotomies" *In Public Folklore*. eds. Robert Baron and Nicholas Spitzer. Washington, London: Smithsonian Institution Press, 1992. Print.

Kluckhohn, William B. "Recurrent Themes in Myths and Mythmaking". *In Proceedings of the American Academy of Arts and Sciences* 882 (1959): 268-79. JSTOR.org/ stable/20026496.

Kumar, B. B. *Folklore & Folklore Motifs (Special reference to North-East)*, New Delhi: Omsons Publications, 1993. Print.

Levi - Strauss, Claude. *Myth and Meaning*. New York: University of Toronto Press, 1978. Print.

-----. "The Structural Study of Myth". *The Journal of American Folklore* 68. 270, Myth: A Symposium (Oct., – Dec., 1955):428-444. University of Illinois Press on behalf of American Folklore Society. Print.

-----. *The Savage Mind.* Trans. By George Weidenfield. London: University of Chicago, Weidenfieed and Nicolson, 1962. Print.

Levin, Harry. "Some Meanings of Myth". *Daedalus* 88. 2 (Spring, 1959): 223-231. Myth and Mythmaking, The MIT Press on behalf of American Academy of Arts & Sciences. Print.

Luyster, Robert. "The Study of Myth: Two Approaches". *Journal of Bible and Religion* 34. 3 (July 1966): 235-243. Oxford University Press, *JSTOR.* Web 17 Feb. 2009.

Longchar, A. Wati. *The Tribal Religious Traditions* (in North East India). Jorhat: Eastern Theological College, 1991. Print.

Malinowski, B. *Sex, Culture and Myth.* London: Harcourt, Brace and world, 1967. Print.

-----. *Myth in Primitive Psychology,* in his *Magic,* Science and Religion. London: W.W. Norton and Company, inc., 1954. Print.

Marak, R Caroline. *Influence on Garo Poetry.* New Delhi: Scholar Publishing House (P) Ltd, 1985. Print.

-----. "Festival and Ceremonies of *Attongs*"; *Festivals and Ceremonies in Meghalaya.* eds. Marak, K.R and R.

Wankhar, Shillong: Department of Art and Culture, 1994. Print.

-----. *Garo Literature*. New Delhi: Sahitya Akademi, (Reprinted) 2004. Print.

-----. "Some Aspects of the *A·chik* Culture in the Brahmaputra Valley" *Rivers and Culture: Focus on Garo Hills*, eds. Marak R Caroline and Sujit Som, Bhopal: IGRMS, 2004. Print.

-----. "Chuganringa or Mangona" *Festivals and Ceremonies in Meghalaya*. eds. Marak K.R and R. Wankhar, Historical and Antiquarian Studies, Department of Arts and Culture, Government of Meghalaya, Shillong, 1994. Print.

Marak, Carvel. "Ganol River and Its Impact on the Lives of the People"; *Rivers and Culture: Focus on Garo Hills*. eds. Marak. R Caroline and Sujit Som, Bhopal: IGRMS, 2004. Print.

Marak, K Fameline. "The Ildek River: Its Myths and Legends"; *Rivers and Culture: Focus on Garo Hills*. eds. Marak R Caroline and Sujit Som, Bhopal: IGRMS, 2004. Print.

Marak, W Harendra. *A·chik Aganbewalrang (Original Tales of the Garos*) (6th Edition). Tura: M.M. Point, 2010. Print.

Marak, R Jacqueline. "River Dareng and Its Role in the Economic Life of South Garo Hills"; *Rivers and Culture: Focus on Garo Hills*, eds. Marak R Caroline and Sujit Som, Bhopal: IGRMS, 2004. Print.

Marak, R Kume. *Traditions and Modernity in Matrilineal Tribal Society.* New Delhi: Inter India Publications, 1997. Print.

Marak, K.R and R Wankhar. *Festivals and Ceremonies in Meghalaya.* Shillong: Department of Art and Culture, 1994. Print.

Marak, L.R. Julius. *Serejing Aro Waljan* (Dakmesokani Bak I, II, III). Mankachar: Rashmi Ideal Printers, 1999. Print.

-----.*Garo Customary Law and Practices* (A Sociological Study). New Delhi: Akansha Publishing House, 2000. Print.

-----. *Balpakram: The Land of the Spirits* (Garo Mythology). New Delhi: Akansha Publishing House, 2000. Print.

-----. "Geology and Geography of the Land and the River Systems with special reference to the Ildek River of East Garo Hills District"; *Rivers and Culture: Focus on Garo Hills.* eds. Marak R Caroline and Sujit Som, Bhopal: IGRMS, 2004. Print.

Marak, R Paulinus. *The Garo Tribal Religious Beliefs and Practices.* Kolkata: Maulana Abul Kalem Azad Institute of Asian Studies, Delhi- Anshah, 2005. Print.

Mathur, Nita. *Alternative Paradigms in Folklore Studies: The Indian Chapter.* Indira Gandhi National Centre for Arts. New Delhi: Janpath, 2001. Print.

Mayes, Clifford. *Ten Pillars of a Jungian Approach to Education* 18.2. (Summer, 2005):

McNeill, William H. "Mythistory, or Truth, Myth, History, and Historians". *The American Historical Review* 91.1 (Feb., 1986):1-10, American Historical Association, *JSTOR*. Web 17 Feb. 2009.

Mercier, Jean L. *Being Human*. Bangalore: Asian Trading Corporation, 1998. Print.

Mibang, Tamo and Sarit K Chaudhuri. *Folk Culture and Oral Literature from North-East India*. New Delhi: Mittal Publications, 2004. Print.

Mildorf, Jarmila. *Sociolinguistic Implications of Narratology: Focalization and 'Double Deixis' in Conversational Story Telling*. University of Stuttgart, 2006. Print.

Momin, Mignonette. *Readings in History and Culture of the Garos* (Essay in honour of Milton S. Sangma). New Delhi: Regency Publications, 2003. Print.

Morrison, James H. "Global Perspective of Oral History in Southeast Asia". *In Oral History in Southeast Asia*, 1998. Print.

Munz, Peter. "History and Myth". *The Philosophical Quarterly* 6. 22(Jan., 1956): 211-222. Blackwell Publishing for the Philosophical Quarterly, *JSTOR*. Web 16 Feb. 2009.

Murray, A Henry. "Introduction to the Issue Myth and Mythmaking". *Daedalus* 88.2 (Spring, 1959): Myth and Mythmaking, The MIT Press on behalf of American Academy of Arts & Sciences, *JSTOR*. Web 17 Feb. 2012.

Narvaez, Peter. The Folklore of 'Old Foolishness': *New foundland Media Legends, Canadian Literature* 108 (Spring, 1986): 125-43. Print.

Pianazzi, A. *In Garoland.* Calcutta: Catholic Orphan Press, 1934. Print.

Peters, Jay. *The Science of Folklore at the end of the 19th Century.* New Jersey: Department of History Rutgers University, 2011. Print.

Pettazzoni, R. *Essay on the History of Religions.* London, 1954. Print.

Playfair, A Major. *The Garos* (2nd Print). Guwahati: Spectrum Publications, 1998. Print.

Polyani, Livia. *Telling the American Story: A Structural and Cultural Analysis of Conversational Storytelling.* Massachusetes: The MIT Press, 1989. Print.

Power, L William. "Myth, Truth and Justification in Religion". *Religious Studies* 22. ¾ (Sept., – Dec., 1986): 447-458, Cambridge University Press. Web 17 Feb. 2009.

Propp, V.J. *Morphology of the Folktale.* Austin: University of Texas Press. (Originally published in Russian as *Morfologiya* Skazhi 1928), Trans in 1968. The American Folklore Society and Indiana Unversity. Print

Rana, B.S. *The People of Meghalaya* (Study on the people and their Religio-cultural life). Calcutta: Punthi Pustak, 1989. Print.

Rimmon-Kenan, Slomith. *Concepts of Narrative.* Helsinki: The Digital Repository of University of Helsinki, 2006. Print.

-----. *Narrative Fiction* (second edition). Routledge, London and New York, 2009. Print.

Rizvi, S.H.M & Shibani Roy. *Garo (A·chik)Tribe of Meghalaya.* Delhi: R.B. Publishing Corporation, 2006. Print.

Roman, Jakobson. "On Realism in Art". *Readings in Russian Poetics: Formalist and Structuralist view* (1971): 38-46. eds. Ladislav Matejka and Krystyna Pomorska. Cambridge, MA: MIT Press, Print.

Rongmuthu, Dewansingh. *The Traditional Dances of the Garos.* Shillong: Singhania Printing Press, 1996. Print.

-----. *Apasong Agana* (As told by my Forefathers). Delhi: Romil, (Reprinted) 1997. Print.

-----. *The Epic Lore of the Garos.* Gauhati: Gauhati University Publication Department, 2008 (Reprint). Print.

-----.*The Folk-Tales of the Garos.* Gauhati: Gauhati University Publication Department, 2008 (Reprint). Print.

-----. *Jadoreng* (The Psycho-Physical Culture of the Garos) (2nd Edition/Reprint). Tura: Students' Book Emporium, 2011. Print.

Ross Murfin and Supiya M. Roy. *The Bradford Glossary of Literary Terms* (second edition). Boston, New York: Bradford/ St. Martin's, 2003. Print.

Roth, Klaus. "*Narration, Narratives and Intercultural Communication*" Folklore New Perspectives. eds. Handoo Jawaharlal Handoo and Reimund Kvideland, Mysore: Zooni Publications, 1999. Print.

Ryan, Marie-Laure. "Beyond Myth and Metaphor: The case of Narrative in digital media." *International journal of computer game research* 1(July 2001): Print.

Ryan, M.L (Editors). *Narrative across Media: The Languages of Storytelling* (1ˢᵗ ed). Lincoln; London: University of Nebraskan Press, 2004. Print.

Sangma, K Dhoronsingh. *A·chik Golporang Bak I* (Garo Folklore 9ᵗʰ Edition). Tura: Tura Book Room, 1988. Print.

-----. *A·chik Golporang Bak II* (Garo Folkore 7ᵗʰ Edition). Tura: Tura Book Room, 1974. Print.

-----. *A·chik Golporang Bak III* (Garo Folklore 3ʳᵈ Edition). Tura: Tura Book Room, 1984. Print.

Sangma, Mihir. *Maniani Bidik* (9ᵗʰ Edition). Tura: Garo Hills Book Emporium, 1995. Print.

-----. *Pagitchamni Ku.bisring* Bak I (2ⁿᵈ Edition). Tura: Eeu Dee Printers, 1996. Print.

-----. "Various forms of festival and ceremonies of the Garos (Ambeng Areas)", *Festivals and Ceremonies in Meghalaya.* eds. Marak K.R and R. Wankhar, Shillong: Historical and Antiquarian Studies, Department of Art and Culture, Government of Meghalaya, Shillong, 1991. Print.

-----. "History, Geology and Economic Importance of the Simsang River"; *Rivers and Culture: Focus on Garo Hills.* eds. Marak R Caroline and Sujit Som, Bhopal: IGRMS, 2004. Print.

Sangma, S Milton. *History and Culture of the Garos.* New Delhi: Oriental Publishers, 1981. Print.

-----. *History of Garo Literature.* NEHU Shillong: Printed at NEHU Printing Press, (Reprinted) 1992. Print.

-----. *Hill Societies.* New Delhi: Omsons Publications, 1995. Print.

-----. "The Concept of Pantheon". *Heritage of Meghalaya* Vol. V (2002-2003): Directorate of Arts and Culture, Govt. Of Meghalaya, Shillong.

Sangma, Simison. *A·chik Golporang* (Garo Folklore 8th Edition). Tura: Tura Book Room, 1984. Print.

Sarma Siddheswar. *Meghalaya –The Land and Forest (A remote sensing base study).* Guwahati: Bhabani offset and Imaging Systems, Pvt. Ltd, 2003. Print.

Schorer, Mark. "The Necessity of Myth". *Daedalus* 88. 2 (Spring, 1959): Myth and Mythmaking, The MIT Press on behalf of American Academy of Arts and Science. Print.

Sen, Soumen. *Folklore in North East India.* New Delhi: Omsons Publications, 1985. Print.

Sharma, Kanak Chandra. "The Brahmaputra and the Rivers of Garo Hills as Reflected in Mythology and

A·chik Folk-Literature"; *Rivers and Culture: Focus on Garo Hills*. eds. Marak R Caroline and Sujit Som, Bhopal: IGRMS, 2004. Print.

Signorlie, Vito. "Acculturation and Myth". *Anthropological Quarterly* 46. 2 (Apr., 1973): 117-134. The George Washington University Institute for Ethnographic Research, *JSTOR*. Web 16 Feb. 2009.

Sinha, Tarunchandra. *The Psyche of the Garos*. Calcutta: Anthropological Survey of India, Government of India, 1966. Print.

Streeter, George L. "Archetypes and Symbolism". *Science* New Series 65.1687 (Apr., 29, 1927): 405-412. American Association for the Advancement of Science, *JSTOR*. Web 17 Feb. 2009.

Thomas, M.C. *Religious Beliefs and Customs Among the Garos*. ed. Sangma, M.S. *Hill Societies Their Modernisation*, New Delhi: Omsons Publications, 1995. Print.

Thomas, F. George. "Myth and Symbol in Religion". *Journal of Bible and Religion* 7. 4 (Nov., 1939): Oxford University Press, *JSTOR*. Web 17 Feb. 2009.

Thompson, Stith. "Motif" *In Standard Dictionary of Folklore, Mythology and Legend*. eds. Maria Leach and Jerome Fried. New York: Funk and Wagnails, 1949-1950. Print.

-----. *Motif Index of Folk-Literature*, 6 (1955-58): Helsinki: Bloomingtone Indiana Press. Print.

Threadgold, T. *"Performing Theories of Narrative: Theorsising Narrative Performance".* The Sociolinguistics of Narrative. Thornborrow, J., Coates, J. (eds). 1ˢᵗ ed. Amsterdam: Philadelphia: John Benjamin's Publishing Company, 2005. Print.

Thury, Eva M and Margaret K. Deviney. *Introduction to Mythology* (2ⁿᵈ Edition). New York: Oxford University Press, 2009. Print.

Tiwari, B.k.Barik, S.K & Tripathi, R. S. *Sacred Forests of Meghalaya – Biological and Cultural Diversity.* Shillong: Regional Centre, National Afforestation and Ecological Development Board, NEHU, 1999. Print.

Todorov, Tzvetan. *The Living Handbook of Narratology.* Hamburg: Interdisciplinary Centre for Narratology, University of Hamburg, 1966. Print.

-----. Communications. Ithaca: Cornell University, 1966. Print.

Todorov Tzvetan and Arnold Weinstein. "Structural Analysis of Narrative". *Novel: A Forum on Fiction* 3.1 (Autumn, 1969): 70-76. Duke University Press, *JSTOR*.org/stable/1345003. Web. 27/1/2009.

Tomascikova, Slavka. "Narrative Theories and Narrative Discourse". *Philology and Cultural Studies*, Bulletin of the Transilvania, University of Brasov 2. 51 (2009): Print.

Treitler, Leo. "History and Archetypes". *Perspectives of New Music* 35.1 (Winter, 1997): 115-127. Perspective of New Music, *JSTOR*. Web 17 Feb. 2009.

Turner, Victor W. *Myth and Symbol.* International Encyclopedia of the Social Science. New York: Crowell Collier and Macmillan, 1968. Print.

Turner, Bryan. *The Sociology of Religion. (The SAGE Handbook of Sociology)*London: SAGE Publications.Clegg. S, 2006. Print.

Vidyarthi, L.P & Binay Kumar Rai. *The Tribal Culture of India.* New Delhi: Concept, Reprinted 1976. Print.

Vidyarthi, L.P. "Folkore Research in India" *In Essays in Indian Folklore.* ed. L.P. Vidharthi. Calcutta: Indian Publications, 1973. Print.

Watre, Thomas Iris. *Music and Musical Instruments of the Garo Tribe of North-East India.* New Delhi: Akansha, 2007. Print.

White, Hayden. The Value of Narrativity in the Representation of Reality. InW.J.T. Mitchell (ed.), *On Narrative.* Chicago: The University of Chicago Press, 1981. Print.

Glossary

A

A·chik - A garo man / hill / hillock

A·chik mande - 'hill men'. The tribe itself is known to outsiders as 'Garo' but the Garos call themselves, '*A·chik - mande*' or 'hill men'. The educated *Garos* of today like to call themselves only as *A·chik*.

A·chik A· song - The Garo Land/ a steep region/ a high place.

A·king – Form or mode of tenure of the hill lands in Garo Hills. *A·king* land means hereditarily held or owned by a *chatchi* or *mahari* whose members cultivate land and settle in a village within the *a·king* land.

A·ning Bokrinima Chining Randinima - Goddess of energy and vitality in the underworld/ *Dikki*'s adopted mother

A·siroka - Sacrificial ceremony performed in the morning after burning the *jhum* field. This chant is done for purification of the farmland, and is also a prayer for blessings.

A·song – Country

Abet – An ancient patriarch and a simpleton amongst the Garos

Abet Rangge – Name of a malicious god of fountain and rills in the Garo pantheon. He is also called *Abet Rora Rakka Ganda* by the *Matchi* division and *Asi* by the *Atong* division of the *A·chik*. Sacrificial offerings, known as *Bisik Krita* by the *Chisak* and *A·we* division of the *A·chiks*, have to be offered to him.

Abilik - A genus of bean

Abong Noga - The Paramount *A·chik* Sovereign

Adil – A long horn made out of buffalo horn which is joined to a long hollow bamboo

Ae Dikante - A destitute widow

Aema Ditema - Mother of fullness and overflowing

Aganmitapa -To state with hidden meaning

Agatchi - Dilennis pentazyna

Ago-Dinggopa - A demi-god

Ahaoea or *Ahaia* - A *wangala* festival and also song of the *Jamegapa* season

Aijangga Reding Banda or *Norimjak Nosiksak* - Creator of all heavenly bodies

Ajea - A kind of song chanted by an individual or by two participants in response to one another

Ajebalsala - A kind of wooing and proposal to enter into love and marriage

Akkal /Bang / Rakasi - The fiend of famine.

Am·beng - Sub-division of the *A·chiks*

Amawari - Brahmaputra

Amrechu - Plantain leaf

Amua - To invoke the deities with due rites; to address in prayer of chanting

Analepsis - Narration of a story-event at a point in the text after later events have been told

Anang and *Dilkang* -The most powerful deities

Anang Nokmong - The deepest pool in the *Ildek* river

Araowaka - A lively song for any occasion

Araru/ bengraru - An order of palm (careya indica)

Arche - Original

Aruak - Name of a village in the eastern part of the Tura range

Ase and *Malja* - Two human representatives deputed to attend the function in order to learn and to peform the *Wangala* on earth but failed to turn up at the function. They are also symbols of disobedience to authority and to cosmic order.

Asima-Dingsima - Mother of those that walk and crawl about the earth.

Atchigittinga - A kind of reincarnation

Atongs - One of the *A·chik* divisions

B

Ba·bra / Rabuga Ranaga - God creator of man

Balpakram - A plateau in the south-east of the district, believed to be the abode of the dead.

Balwa - The fleetest and the finest looking man among the A·chik heroes.

Bandi - The strongest, the bravest and the most alert warrior among the A·chik heroes.

Banggal rori - A term used by *A·chiks* to refer to non- tribals.

Bangji Me·chik - The wife of *Dema Resi Eman Me·a.*

Bengbul - A frog

Bidawe - A spirit that steals the soul of men

Bilcham - Traditional torches

Bolchim - Duabanga sonnetatioides

Boldak - Schima Wallichii

Bolong - Cyathocalyx martabanicus

Bone Nirepa Jane Nitepa - the man who is said to have pioneered *jhum* cultivation, whose first field was *Misi Kokdok A·bri* (the Hill of Six Basketfuls of Millet) in the north-east of Garo Hills.

Burungni mite - Deity of the jungle

But – Spirit

C

Cha·chat Soa - Burning of the Incense

Chaging - A late variety of rice

Chama - Astocarpus chaplasha

Chambuni - A herb inducing sleep and also the name of a *A·chik* matriarch

Chando - A merchant-prince

Chatchi - Clan

Chekke - Coop-like nets made from slit bamboo especially meant for catching prawns, crabs and small fish / triangular fishing basket

Chela Asanpa and Brara - Living Beings who 'First Acquired Steel'

Chenggari - A kind of cicada

Chera sola - Folk song sung in the *Gara-ganching* area only and the subject of this song is usually about heroic deeds of the heroes and heroines.

Chibok - White stream of water

Chidimak Chikong - The black or sooty stream of water. The *A·chiks* cremate their dead on funeral pyres of dried wood from time immemorial past. It is believed that the spirits of the dead used to take their ceremonial dips in a particular inky stream of water.

Chigat - A bathing place

Chiginap Rongjamdap Chibrasni Chongsni - Place of the confluence of seven streams of water

Chikmang /Balmang - An isolated hill in the South Garo Hills and is considered as the dwelling place of god almighty giver of human lives

Chiring - Stream/ rivulet

Chondodenga - A Hillock in *A·chik* land

Chorabudi - A benign spirit , protector of crops

Chras - A woman's brother or maternal uncle

Chugan - A term for post funeral ceremony used by *Atongs* (*A·chik* subdivision)

D

Dakdame - The goddess of vitality and strength

Dakkara - The deity of creation

Dakgipa Rugipa - the Maker, the Moulder

Dal·gipa Nalsa - Great Beyond

Damra / Cheran - Place in the north-eastern hills

Dani Doka - A traditional *A·chik* song sung to a tune by elderly men, to the exclusion of women and young men. The singing of the *Dani* is a feature of the *Wangala* festival of harvest and thanksgiving to the gods

Den·bilsia or *A·a bakchata* - Ceremony of clearing the jungles for *jhum* cultivation, signifying the driving off of all uncleanness and disease.

Dengreng Kitik Wari Chora - Watering-place of *Dimrimpa Dimsimpa Gaeripa Singeripa*, the ancient patriarch of *Mande* (man), who was the first to taste death among humankind and is sacred to the *A·chiks*

Dikge - Tuberous herb of medicinal value of the order of the ginger and turmeric

Dikki - The wisest of the *A·chik* heroes

Dimbil - Careya arborea

Dime ring·a - A song sung in *Atong* area

Dingipa Babra Mugipa Jaring - Divine Mother and the great mathematical thinker, who has also fashioned the size, height, looks and constitution of each living person

Do·aran - A kind of bird

Do·bik - Entrails of the fowl

Do·biknia - To consult the omens with the help of the entrails of the fowl

Do·chi goa - Breaking eggs

Do·grik - Black pheasant

Do·mesal - Species of wild fowl

Do·sia - *A·chik* traditional marriage ceremony

Do·sisi - A kind of bird

Do·uang - A night-jar or a bird which is believed to call out at night when a person is going to die, its cry denotes the death of a person.

Doancheng - A kind of bird with white breast

Dore - White-headed babbler

Doroa - A chant to celebrate the house warming

Dura hills - The ancient Garo name for the Tura Range in Garo Hills.

Durama Imbama - Literally, the Mother of *Dura*, the Grand and Majestic, and the Mother of *Imba*, the profoundly potent. The tutelary Goddess of *A·chikland* in the Garo pantheon, who is represented by the *Dura* Hills in Garo Hills.

G

Gaanti - A kind of cicada

Gan·drak - A kind of green frog

Gana - Woman's dress

Gangbo Nokma - A rich man named *Gangbo*

Gangsime Gangchime /renggok bima - The female hornbill

Ganol - One of the largest rivers in Garo Hills, originating in the Tura range near Tura

Gasampe - A tree with edible fruits

Ghat - River bank

Ghost *Bogia* - Demon

Gilmrong/ Kilmrong - A 'Y' shaped post planted upright near the place of cremation where a bull is kept tethered before it is being killed / a sacrificial post

Ginde gala – First fruit offering ceremony in *Wangala* festival

Gnarus - Signifiers

Goera - God of thunder and lightning, of strength and protection.

Gogaia, Gosaia - A folk song

Gonda Doka - Folk song on nature and on human theme

Gonga - The man who first taught the *A·chiks* to make thread for clothing

Grapmangtata /Kabe /Grapmikchi - Funeral wails

Gukchru - A kind of green locust

Gure - A horse

J

Ja·megapa or *Megap ra·ona* - A special ceremony performed during the reaping of the jhum paddy.

Jabirong - It is a secret *A·chik* doctrine of conscious trans- incarnation of the human *jachri* or *jabirong. Jabirong* means self-active, self-mobile, self-projecting

Jachri - self-acting, self-propelling.

Jamegapa - The initial post-harvest thanksgiving ceremony

Jangekoknal Damal – A place in East Garo Hills

Jaoka/Jaringa /Chidema - Means 'retrieving' the straying human psyche

Jaru Me·a Jabal Pante Okkuangsi Ja·patchongsi - The god of Winds

Jati - A kind of bamboo

Jhum - Shifting cultivation

Jingjang, Nongdu a·ding pante, Gangga and *Rutha* – The heroes and heroines of the *A·chiks*

Jinjiram river- A tributary of the Brahmaputra river

K

Kalkame - He is the elder brother of Goera and is the caretaker of all men on earth.

Kalkame Kalgra - Literally it means the Being whose Presence one always feels. The Invisible but Presence Felt, Guardian Spirit or Angel in the *A·chiks* pantheon, who is also called one's own Gosain, the god of daemon, who keeps watch at all times over one's person and life or the divinity who follows a person just as his or her shadow does/ the god of destiny

Kalu river - Another name for Ganol river

Kamal - A priest

Kangse Tira - A destitute

Katchi Beari - The Celestial messenger

Katta Agangipa - A narrator

Katta Salling - Narrative of Salling

Kera - A small bakset

Kilbolma - The gigantic cotton tree

Kima - Memorial post erected in front and outside of the house for the memory of the deceased member of the family.

Kimde - Mesua ferrea

Kitma - Rhus semialata

Kok – A bamboo basket carried suspended from the head with a flat string made from bark of certain trees

Koksep - A bamboo basket with a lid

Koksi - A bamboo basket used to store prawns, crabs, small fish, cockles etc. while looking for the same in the stream

Kram, Kram achok / kram bichok - A kind of drum used for rituals to the gods. It is hewn out of *gambare* tree (Gmelina arborea) by persons authorised by the gods. A specimen *kram* measures 84 cms in length, the diameter at the larger end is 16 cms and the diameter at the narrow end is 6½ cms. The ends are covered with hide. When it is completed, animal sacrifice is performed inorder to consecrate it before it is taken into the house of nokma. No woman dances with the *kram* player because the god of the kram dwells in it.

Ku·gri - A dumb person

Kumanchi Wal·dukaa - A negotiation between God and humankind

L

Lau – Pitcher or jug made out of the shell of 'lau' or bottle gourd

Logos - Speech, oration, discourse, quote, study, reason and argument

M

Ma·ambi - A narrative to trace the geneology

Ma·chong - Ancestry

Machi - Lesser spirits

Maldengong - A mythical animal

Manda - Another name for Dudhnoi river

Mandal - Erythrina Suberosa

Manggual - The house or the place where a corpse of a person who meets with unnatural death is kept

Mangona - A post funeral ceremony (Chugan in Atong)

Mangru- Mangram - A kind of purgatory through which all must pass good and the bad alike after their death

Märchen –Folktale / fairy tale

Matabeng - Sub-division of the *A·chiks*

Matchadu or *Dudurong* - A tiger man; a creature that is a man during the day and a tiger at night.

Matma - Buffalo

Matta - A wooden stick pointed at one end used for making holes in the ground for putting seeds in hill paddy cultivation

Me·gam Gairipa - *Gairipa* literally means "the father of *Gairi*" the suffix – pa is usually put to denote that he is the father of the person whose name is suffixed. The *A·chiks* address married men by the names of their first born and adding the suffix/ the first man to taste death among human beings

Mande Singeripa -The father of *Singeri* - the first man to taste death among human beings

Me·gong - Barebinia variegata

Me·jak - Rythymeokchina

Me·jak sim·a - An offering to the deity of crops so that she may protect the crops from every possible destruction caused by insects, moths, animals, failure of rain

Me·mang - Ghost / spirit

Me·mang Bugini Ja·nengtakram and *Katchini Janepani Kasperam* - Resting place of Spirit of *Bugi* and *Katchi-Janepa*

Me·mang Mesal Cha·ram - A place in Balpakram where the spirits eat their midday meal

Me·gam -A sub-division of the *A·chiks*

Memang Ra·rika - The process of keeping the spirit of the dead at home

Meminram -Peak of the Dura Range

Mikkol - Name of the infatuated monkey. *Mik* stands for eye and *kol* for hole or depression. Evidently it suggests the depression like eye sockets of the monkey.

Mil·am - double-edged sword used by the *A·chiks* for both warfare and in certain ceremonies.

Minimaa Rokkime - The mother of rice and Goddess of wealth, the ideal personification of all that is beauteous, auspicious, desired and desirable in worldly terms.

Misi Kokdok Abri - The name of a hill in East Garo Hills meaning six baskets of millet.

Misi Saljong - The sun god, who first taught humankind the art of cultivation and also provided seed grains to humankind/ god of food crops.

Mitdemechik - Goddess

Mite - A deity/ a spirit

Mite chika - Spirit bites or bite of the Spirit.

Moepa - The resplendent sun

Monaretchi - Banana fibre

Mune and *Sane* - Daughters of an *A·chik* forefather who practiced jhum cultivation.

Munepa -An *A·chik* forefather

Muni - A herb inducing sleep

Mythos - Narrative, speech, word, fact, and story

N

Na·chi - A kind of fresh water fish

Na·ma Na·sa - The mother of fish

Nanggore - A folk song for all happy occasions

Napak - The dwelling place of the spirits of the dead

Nawang -A demon which devours the souls of men

Niba Jonja - The first man to have acquired the *muni* and *chambuni* (a herb inducing sleep)

Nitai - the River that originates from the majestic *Nokrek* range in central Garo Hills and is known as *Dareng* by the *A·chiks*.

Nokma - It has seven meanings, namely: (i) one who keeps the *a·king* land of his village on behalf of the *chatchi* or *mahari* to which his wife belongs. Such *Nokma* is known as *A·king Nokma*. (ii) One who is wealthy, such a *Nokma* is known as *Nokdangni Nokma* or *Gamni Nokma*. (iii) One who has performed the expensive *Gana* ceremony. Such a *Nokma* is known *Miteni*

Nokma. (iv) One who is hereditarily in the position of a Chieftain or king. Such a *Nokma* is known as *Bakapaonin Nokma.* (v) One who is appointed a village – headman by the government so that he may help the government officials in the discharge of their various duties within the village domain. Such a *Nokma* is known as *Sorkarini Nokma.* (vi) One, who for visible manifestations of qualities of heart and head in word or deed, is a well-known and respected both by the public in general and the government. Such a *Nokma* is known as *Chalang Nokma.* (vii) One, who for his deep erudition in the divinities, mythological lore and mysterious profundities of creation, is generally looked up to as a visible source of spiritual enlightenment by his own people. Such a *Nokma* is called *Kamal Nokma.*

Nokma Abong Chirepa - The last independent and Paramount Highland Chieftain in the Hills.

Nokni mite - A deity that resides in the house

Nokrek - The highest peak of Tura range

Norebak Norekdim and *Jipjini Japjana* - God creator of all living beings on earth and the ocean

Noro - The first human being to inhabit the Earth.

Nosari Bandari - The abode of two water-nymphs

Nostu Nopantu Misi Siste - Deity who separated the land from water.

Nostu-Nopantu - Deity, who at the command of *Tatara-Rabuga*, fashioned the earth

O

O·pata -To select a portion of the jungle for *jhum* cultivation by cutting some trees and shrubs

Olmak - Sterculia villosa – a species of tree. Its bark is used as belts to hang the wicker baskets from the head.

Opsoras or *mitdemechik* - Goddesses/ Celestial damsel. The *A·chiks* believe that *Opsoras* or *mitdemechik* (goddess) are perfectly human in forms and features and dressed in snow-white clothes. They are reputed to be bewitchingly beautiful and capable of seducing young men by means of their charms. The *A·chiks* believe that the *Opsoras* are fond of bathing in lonely crystal clear pools or lakes, especially on tops of high hills, during cloudless summer days. They are believed to be immortal beings.

P

Poi - An utterance which accompanies the spitting out of water, signifying purification of the plot cleared for cultivation

Pong - Shell of small variety of gourd used for ladling and serving rice beer

Prolepsis – A narration of a story-event before earlier events have been mentioned

R

Rama Cholsni - The parting of seven path ways

Rang - Basin-like lead-brass gongs/ ceremonial gongs

Ranggira - A hill, 2205 feet in height, to the west of Tura town

Re - A cane

Rechu or *amrechu* - A plantain leaf

Rere Ring·a - An indigenous romantic *A·chik* song sung by the *Rugas*, the *Duals* and the *Chiboks* of the *A·chik* subdivision

Rime-Rinok -The patriarchial head of the land-lizards or iguanas

Ringchanchok - The 'leaning boat'

Ringgi - Tributary of the river *Ganol*

Dilni - Tributary of the river *Ganol*

Risi - The deity who is associated with a particular *kram* (drum)

Rokkime - The mother of food grains of rice

Rong·dikni mite - The deity of the rice storage vessel

Rongchu Gala or *Ginde Gala* – First fruit offering ceremony

Rongribo and *Kalak* - village on the upper reaches of the *Damring* river

Rongro Rongkimjeng Chiancheng Dasreng – The homes of the *sangknis*

Rurime Todik - The goddess who moulds human forms and is identified with the Sun-Myth

Rusrota - The last ceremony of the year/ libation

S

Sae-Dina-Mangga-Dine - God of death

Sal tree - Shorea robusta

Salaram Mitechak - The divine Sanctuary of the East/ place where present day Kamakhya Temple is located.

Salchame - A kind of wild bird

Salgira / Salgra - The sun god

Saljong - The moon god; the god of fertility and crops

Sane - Daughter of an *A·chik* forefather who practiced jhum cultivation

Sangknis - Aquatic serpents of immense size, measuring from two hundred fifty to three hundred cubits in length. The big deep pools in large rivers owe their depth to the presence of these gigantic aquatic serpents; that deep pools become silted up with sand.

These serpents are very much afraid of *Goera*, the God of thunder and lightning.

Seng·ki - A gridle made of several strings of beads worn by women

Serejing - A folk song popular with the *A·chik* young man and woman

Setiri or *badagong* - An extremely variable scant perennial climber

Simera – Daughter of *Durama Imbama*

Simram - Immersion place

Simsang - The *Someswari* river, the biggest in Garo Hills

Simul - Cotton tree (bombax malabaricum)

Singra - The son of mother *Songdu*

Sjuzet - The organization of events in the text

Songdu - A Garo name for Brahmaputra

Songduma- Rekbokchiga - The great sea

Songduma- Sagalma - Mother of oceans

Spi - Rectangular shield made of cane wicker or carved from wood.

Sre-Tonggitchak-Gitok-Warikat - The mother of the god of fire

Susime - A female deity, the giver of both good and bad things to mankind / Moon god

Tatara Rabuga - God who created the Universe.

Stura Pantura - the Sole knot and Cohesion of existence

T

Te·dambil - A village on the banks of the *Ildek* river

Tilta - A 'Y' shaped post planted upright near the place of cremation where a bull is kept tethered before it is killed / a sacrificial post.

Toban - Warrior-hero

Tongrengma - A female deity, who has the power to cause ailment to human lives

Truma or *Turumal* - The central post of the house

Tuai! Tuai! - An act and sound of spitting to show one's contempt

Typos - Form or model.

W

Wa·dro - A kind of bamboo

Wa·ge Marang – A place near Papera Hill, bordering Khasi Hills, falling on the *Me·gam* area

Waimong - King of death; *Wai* - the king of the spirits; *Mong* - important more than all the other spirits/ the care taker of the land of the spirits.

Wangala/ Drua Wanbola / Wanna rongchua – The harvest festival. It is a 'thanksgiving' as well as 'Send-off-ceremony' to bid farewell to *Minimaa Rokkime* (mother of paddy) and *Misi Saljong* (god of food crops)

Wari - Pools

Watpaka - A sent off at the time of cremation, practised by *Am·beng* and *Matabeng* (sub-division of the *A·chiks*)

Weram Jambil - A small hillock close to *Jambal gittim* in *Rongjeng* in the north-eastern part of Garo Hills.

Appendix

SONGDU OR AMAWARI OR BRAHMAPUTRA

GANOL RIVER DURING 2014 FLOOD

BALPAKRAM

CHITMANG

TILTA

KIMA

DIKGE

CHIDIMAK

Printed in the United States
By Bookmasters